THOMAS COLE'S
POETRY

THE COLLECTED POEMS OF AMERICA'S
FOREMOST PAINTER OF THE HUDSON RIVER SCHOOL
REFLECTING HIS FEELINGS FOR NATURE
AND THE ROMANTIC SPIRIT
OF THE NINETEENTH CENTURY

By

THOMAS COLE

Compiled and Edited

By

MARSHALL B. TYMN

LIBERTY CAP BOOKS

YORK · PENNSYLVANIA

Book design and production editing
by Janet Gray Crosson

Composed in Aldine Roman on an IBM Selectric Composer
Printed in the United States of America by
W & M Printing of Mechanicsburg, Pa.
Bound by Murphy-Parker Inc. of Philadelphia, Pa.

LIBERTY CAP BOOKS

an imprint of

GEO. SHUMWAY PUBLISHER
R. D. 7, York, Pa. 17402

ABSTRACT

Thomas Cole is well known as the artist who founded the Hudson River School of romantic landscape painting during the 1820's. Through his paintings he called attention to the glories of nature and the American landscape at a time when too many still looked to the Old World for inspiration.

Cole wrote both prose and poetry in addition to his work on canvas, but the literary efforts have remained relatively unknown. In the course of his twenty-five year career Cole composed more than one hundred poems dealing mainly with his feelings about nature. A few of these were put in polished form and were published. Most of the poems, however, have remained in his journals and notebooks, in the rough, and until now have remained unpublished.

This book holds the bulk of Cole's poetic efforts—105 pieces. The collection is unique in allowing the student of the American romantic period to know an important early spokesman through the words of poetry as well as through his painting.

Dedicated

to my

Mother and Father

CONTENTS

POEMS

Manuscript location or source:
- A. New York State Library
- B. Detroit Institute of Arts
- C. Knickerbocker Magazine
- D. Louis L. Noble: THE LIFE AND WORKS OF THOMAS COLE

ILLUSTRATIONS

Cover illustration:
IN THE CATSKILLS
1827
Collection of the Arnot Art Museum
Elmira, New York

PREFACE

This book is an outgrowth of my dissertation completed at the University of Michigan in the summer of 1970, at which time Thomas Cole was receiving increased attention from art historians. I felt that by collecting, editing and remarking on his substantial body of poetry, one could provide the general public as well as students of American literature and art with another basis for evaluating and reacting to Cole.

He was a romantic thinker expounding on his world view in several media. Students of the early Romantic Period of American literature can benefit from studying Cole's nature poems in conjunction with the more readily recognized work of his close friend and contemporary, William Cullen Bryant. And certainly art historians will find the expressions of Cole, the poet, invaluable in reassessing the works of the artist.

The sheer volume of his verse reveals he was not content to limit his creative energies to landscape painting. He wrote poetry for more than two decades before the first of three poems published during his lifetime appeared in print.

The majority of his poems deal with nature themes. Fortunately, a portion of the poems Cole himself dated in manuscript. It is possible to assign approximate dates to others based upon supporting evidence from Cole's journals and letters. The remainder are arranged by title, and where untitled, by first line.

For the most part, the poems have been left intact, retaining Cole's original spelling and occasional inconsistencies of punctuation. References to variant words and phrases written by Cole, and my notes to the poems begin on page 203. Incomplete poems or fragments are not included.

Marshall B. Tymn

ACKNOWLEDGEMENTS

In preparing this work I have profited from the aid and advice of many individuals whose services no words of appreciation could adequately describe. The staffs of the New York State Library and of the Research Library of the Detroit Institute of Arts were most helpful during the period in which papers of Thomas Cole were being studied.

Special thanks are extended to Dr. Marvin Felheim of the University of Michigan, who was ready at all times with useful suggestions involving the preparation of the manuscript, and Dr. David C. Huntington of the University of Michigan, who first suggested this project to me, and whose guidance in researching the field of art history was invaluable. Credit also goes to my wife, Darlene, for her assistance in transcribing the poems and in preparing early drafts of this manuscript.

14

INTRODUCTION

The growth of romantic thought in America was stimulated by the spirit of nationalism which dominated the fine arts during the first half of the nineteenth century. In the aftermath of a newly-acquired political freedom, America had begun to turn its attention inward toward the expansion of the frontier and the exploration of its spectacular landscape, discovering in the process a wellspring of patriotic and romantic impulses in the surrounding wilderness. The intense pride associated with these scenic discoveries was evident in the literary and artistic expressions of poets, essayists, novelists and painters, who took advantage of nature as a resource and vehicle for romantic motifs. With the publication of "Thanatopsis" in 1817, William Cullen Bryant became the first major American poet to utilize indigenous materials in nature poetry. Washington Irving described the picturesque charm of the Catskill mountain region in his SKETCH BOOK, and James Fenimore Cooper's Leatherstocking novels conveyed the sense of grandeur inherent in America's virgin forests and mountain lakes. Concurrently, Thomas Cole, with his interpretations of nature in its wildest form, initiated and provided stimulus to the first native school of artists, who promptly capitalized on the awesome spectacle of a landscape untouched by civilization. The development of landscape painting by the Hudson River School paralleled literary trends during the second quarter of the nineteenth century. There existed close associations between many of the literary and artistic figures of the day.

As a youth in England, Cole had developed an appreciation of nature through his reading of the romantic poets Byron and Wordsworth. Before his departure from England he was apprenticed as an engraver of calico designs. Later, after his family had settled in Steubenville, Ohio, he designed patterns in his father's wallpaper shop and worked as a wood engraver. But, more intrigued by the art of painting, Cole left home to apprentice himself to an itinerant portrait painter who instructed him in the rudiments of canvas and brush. While earning a meager living in this manner, Cole dabbled in landscapes, developing his own techniques by imitating what he had observed in nature. He subsequently moved to Philadelphia, where he received more formal training at the Pennsylvania Academy of Fine Arts.

In 1825 Cole opened his New York studio and soon sold three landscapes, *The High Falls of the Kaaterskill, View of Fort Putnam,* and *Lake with Dead Trees,* to the distinguished patrons, William Dunlap, Asher Durand and Jonathan Trumbull. His career as a landscape painter had begun. That same year Cole wrote a substantial number of nature poems, perhaps his first, and published a short story, "Emma Moreton, a West Indian Tale," in THE SATURDAY EVENING POST. As his reputation as a painter grew, Cole's literary output continually complemented his pictorial renderings of the American landscape.

Cole's earliest writings show an appreciation for wild nature. His concept of nature was, in part, colored by his reliance on the principles of the sublime, which, when interpreted in terms of American scenery, emphasized the dramatic power and magnificence of mountains, waterfalls, forests and lakes. His years on the Ohio frontier had conditioned him to nature in its unspoiled state. When he arrived in the New York region he was quickly enticed by the luxuriant Catskill mountains. During the next few years he made several excursions through its wildest territory.

> He was an untiring walker and discovered, to his ever increasing delight, the unending variety of hills and dales, woods and streams which were still close enough to the frontier to have remained in a state of almost unbroken wilderness. The country was so dear to him because there was always a new horizon beyond the last . . . After a day's rambles, Cole would write down [his impressions] of the scenes and incidents witnessed, or express in verse a thought or sentiment. It became an axiom with him that 'to walk with nature as a poet' was the necessary condition of a perfect artist.[1]

Observations from these expeditions resulted in Cole's literary work titled "Essay on American Scenery" where he surveys the major features of nature, beginning with the mountains, which, he writes, "are the most conspicuous objects in landscape."[2]

To the artist they were symbols of "eternal majesty, immutability and repose." Most of Cole's paintings have mountain backgrounds, and mountain scenery is a dominant element in his verse. The opening lines of "To Mount Washington" (page 49), for example, convey his feelings of awe and reverence. The towering grandeur of mountains was further accentuated in his painting by juxtaposition of diminutive figures against them. This technique is evident both in his religious works and in his purely landscape composition.[3] "These and other paintings," says Roderick Nash, "broke with landscape painting tradition by either omitting any sign of man and his works or reducing the human figure to ant-like proportions. Wilderness dominated the canvas."[4]

Cole places his mountains against a violent sky, broken by storms and clouds, amidst shades of light and dark. This powerful chiaroscuro effectively emphasizes the contrasting extremes found in nature. Dramatic contrast became one of the most typical and striking features of Cole's art. In verse, too, he employs the technique to intensify the elements of the sublime:

> A lonely cloud is flitting round the brow
> Of the dark barren mountain; but the glow
> Of the unrisen sun illumes each fold
> Transmuting blackness into living gold — [5]

Cole also looked upon the mountain, in its remoteness, as a final retreat "from man's impure resort . . . /From turmoil and from dust." This Wordsworthian view of nature as fundamentally benevolent and antithetical to the inherent corruption of civilization is seen in the poem on page 202.

William Cullen Bryant recognized Cole's intense love for

mountains, and refers to his mountains as "unmistakably American" because they were always covered with so many trees. Cole was particularly fond of the changing colors of the October forest.

> There is one season when the American forest surpasses all the world in gorgeousness—that is the autumnal;—then every hill and dale is riant in the luxury of color—every hue is there, from the liveliest green to the deepest purple—from the most golden yellow to the intensest crimson. The artist looks despairingly upon the glowing landscape, and in the old world his truest imitations of the American forest, at this season, are called falsely bright, and scenes in Fairy Land.[6]

This profusion of color invaded the works of both Cole, the landscape painter, and Cole, the nature poet. Two striking examples of his use of the fall colors for dramatic contrast are *The Clove, Catskills* (1827) and *Schroon Mountain* (1838). He focuses on the brilliant hues of the autumnal season in several poems, most notably "Written in Autumn," page 90.

The countless forests that covered the American continent ultimately became the victims of industrial progress. For Cole, trees symbolized most forcibly nature's last stand against the ravages of civilization. A sincere expression of the loss he felt as a witness to the gradual disappearance of the forest is embodied in an 1834 poem, "On seeing that a favorite tree of the Author's had been cut down —," page 67. The poem is an appeal for the preservation of one of nature's miracles; Cole's elaboration of this one small incident reveals the depth of his love and concern for all living things.

Another external feature of nature that Cole emphasizes in his visual and verbal creations is water. Unlike trees, a lake is dependent upon the objects that surround it for changes in its color and character.[7] And unlike the forests, which were being ruthlessly and senselessly destroyed by man, water still remained untouched. Cole stood in awe of the tremendous power generated by the waterfalls of North America. Water as a symbol of strength, its "roaring power suggesting the [wild] forces of nature," is the theme of "Niagara," page 50, written during the author's first visit to the falls shortly before his departure for Europe in June, 1829:

Approach and view the wonder of a world
See! when the waters of a hundred lakes
An unheaped multitude tumultuous leap
O'er the projecting crags, into the gulf —
Thence the thick mist perpetual ascends,
In cloudy piles into the sky and hides,
The quivering torment of the floods below —
Like steam emitted from some cauldron vast
Vexed by furious and unquenching fires —

It is to be expected that water invaded Cole's landscapes as well. Waterfalls were the subjects of two paintings, *Kaaterskill Falls* (1826) and *Distant View of the Falls of Niagara* (c. 1829), and they were an important element in *Landscape with Tree Trunks* (1827), *A Wild Scene* (1831-32) and *Mountain Landscape with Waterfall* (1847). These paintings illustrate Cole's belief in the totality of nature. Mountains, trees and water were all integral, meaningful components of a landscape; together they produced a harmonious, if sometimes precarious, balance in nature.

The crowning touch was always a magnificent sky. Whether it was filled with dark, turbulent storm clouds or with a swirling, pastel cirrus formation at sunset, Cole termed the sky "the soul of all scenery."

Whatever expression the sky takes, the features of the landscape are affected in unison, whether it be the serenity of the summer's blue, or the dark tumult of the storm.[8]

The sky at sunset held a special enchantment for Cole. The sunset, which spread a veil of peace over the earth, brought with it the quietude the artist so dearly loved. During one of his solitary walks through the forest paths which surrounded his house at Catskill, he composed his tender poem, "Twilight":

> The woods are dark; but yet the lingering light
> Spreads its vast beauty o'er the sunset sky
> How lovely are the portals of the night
> When stars come forth to watch the daylight die.
>
> The woods are dark; but yet yon little bird
> Is warbling by his newly furnished nest.
> No.sound beside in all the vale is heard;
> But he for rapture cannot — cannot rest.

Although Cole had joined with Americans in celebrating the wonders of their environment, at the same time he reminds us in his poetic and pictorial descriptions of nature that we live in a universe created by God. Perhaps his most poignant expression of the idea that God's presence is manifest in nature is "Hope and Trust Spring from the Contemplation of the Works of God," page 76, in which the artist's spiritual self is enlarged through a sense of holy communion. Cole incorporates into his landscapes a sterner, harsher view of God than is seen in his poetry. *John the Baptist Preaching in the Wilderness* (1827), *The Expulsion from the Garden of Eden* (1827-28) and *Moses on the Mount* (c. 1828) are among his most sincere efforts at what he calls a "higher style of landscape." It is a style which portrays Biblical subjects against backdrops of rugged mountains, dark clouds and impenetrable chasms. "His conception of Divinity," says Gerdts, "represented pictorially in the surging display of natural forces, is one of drama, often of violence, with Man relegated to a position of insignificance."[9]

As Cole searched for truth among nature's marvels, he came to believe that "there is in the human mind an almost inseparable connection between the beautiful and the good."[10] American scenery, then, could be appreciated not only for its external beauty or its spiritual revelation, but for its espousal of Christian virtues. Seeking moral themes of universal application was a corollary of

Cole's belief in the transcendental world of nature.[11]

In his later years, Cole was preoccupied with the theme of the perishability of man's works. In his five-part series, *The Course of Empire* (1836), he expresses his awareness of the transitory nature of civilization by contrasting the world of man to the far more enduring world of nature. Donald A. Ringe has summarized the moral implications of the series: "The empire itself . . . represents the pride which man takes in his material accomplishments, while the ruin which follows indicates the folly of man's earthly ambitions."[12]

If civilization was ephemeral, man himself was no less so. Cole brooded over the brevity of human life. The fading light at dusk in "Evening Thoughts," page 78, reminds us

> That we are mortal and the latter day
> Steals onward swiftly, like the unseen winds
> And all our years are clouds that quickly pass away.

Significantly Cole chose the occasion of his birthday or the beginning of a new year to comment on the fleeting moments of man's earthly existence. In "Written on my Birthday, Feb. 1, 1830," page 54, the artist laments that life might end before he can achieve artistic fame. Indeed, at his death he left unfinished a selection of poems he was correcting for publication.[13]

Edgar P. Richardson has remarked that "the elegiac note of meditation upon the flight of time and the brevity of human life was a fundamental of the Romantic spirit."[14] With the passing of time, Cole sees a great moral lesson in the pattern of man's life. In his Bunyanesque allegory, "Life's Pilgrimage," page 137, man's existence on earth becomes a series of pitfalls and temptations which he must overcome before he can win everlasting glory. In *The Voyage of Life* (1840), Cole develops the same theme in four pictures: *Childhood, Youth, Manhood* and *Old Age,* which depict man travelling over the "stormy sea of life" toward his final goal, eternal peace.

Contemplating the passage of time inevitably led to a romantic fascination with the past. Cole's reverie upon the past is expressed most sympathetically in what Richardson calls his elegiac land-scapes.[15] *The Roman Campagna* and *An Evening in Arcady* were both completed in 1843 after the artist's second visit to Italy. Most of the ruins that Cole incorporated into his scenes from antiquity were taken from Italian models, there being no such relics in the United States. His contemporaries, likewise, introduced European architectural elements into landscapes clearly American in origin. American scenery, however, was not completely devoid of historical associations. An 1826 poem, "Lines on Lake George," page 45, recalls the horrors of the massacre near Fort William Henry, one of the many bloody conflicts that took place on the shores of that lake during the French and Indian Wars. For the most part, references to the past in Cole's poems are restricted to the frequent use of Biblical and classical names, which he successfully combines with wilderness imagery to evoke the picturesque charm of "remote times and places."[16]

To his study of nature Cole brought a view of the wilder side of romanticism. Bryant's *Funeral Oration* is apt testimony to the particular appeal which Cole's works had for his contemporaries:

> I well remember what an enthusiasm was awakened by these early works of his, . . . the delight which was expressed at the opportunity of contemplating pictures which carried the eye over scenes of wild grandeur peculiar to our country, over our serial mountain-tops with their mighty growth of forest never touched by the axe, along the banks of streams never deformed by culture, and into the depths of skies bright with the hues of our own climate; such skies as few but Cole could ever paint, and through the transparent abyss of which it seemed that you might send an arrow out of sight.[17]

Cole's success as an artist can be attributed, in part, to his systematic approach to a specific art form—landscape painting. His dedication to his art is evident not only in his landscape masterpieces and in the recognition he has received from art historians, but also in his own ad-mission of earnestness expressed in his journals and published writings.

Cole's poetry, on the other hand, has never received noteworthy attention. He was obviously aware of the methods employed by the romantic poets, just as he was aware of their philosophies. As a close analysis of his poems will reveal, Cole continually experimented with meter, stanzaic patterns, rhyme schemes, figurative language, rhythm and poetic devices. He depended upon diversified poetic conventions in his attempt to write romantic poetry, because for him poetry, like the visual arts, was a vehicle for great variety of expression. But his poetic style is generally little more than a conglomeration of romantic techniques.

Cole as poet does not often achieve the "higher style" seen in his paintings. The poems, for the most part, approximate casual diary entries because of their high incidence of topical material. Often, a poem is simply an elaboration of a journal entry. All of these things tend to give a dilettantish quality to the poems and suggest that he did not take this form of creativity seriously. There is no evidence, for example, that Cole took notes for the purpose of writing poetry; nor are there comments in his journals and letters on the obstacles he might have encountered as a poet. In contrast to his paintings, his poems are not meticulous, finished products. Thus Cole's poetry lacks sophistication in comparison with the carefully wrought compositions of his contemporary, Bryant.

It is doubtful that Cole intended his works in their unrefined state to be subjected to such close scrutiny. How *did* Cole view his own poetical efforts? What potential did *he* foresee for them? It is not difficult for the reader to speculate that for one so frequently inspired by his surroundings, poetry indeed provided a second and spontaneous avenue of expression removed from the more disciplined atmosphere his primary vocation imposed upon him. If Cole had been free of the pressures of commissions, exhibition deadlines and the general persistence his painting demanded of him to maintain his status (and thus his livelihood), might he have nurtured his literary talents sufficiently to gain public recognition as a poet?

There are several indications which support such a hypothesis. A large body of poems written over a twenty-five year period had been preserved by Cole and his friends. In the few years prior to his death at the age of forty-seven, he was accepted in the literary world as a spokesman on aesthetics. At the same time his poems began to appear in print.

Cole's informal approach to the craft of poetry does not negate its worth as a necessary guide to his romantic philosophies. One of the chief characteristics of romantic poetry was the sense of variety it embodied. A diversified, individualistic, subjective approach to life ultimately led to a revelation of all that was good and beautiful and true. Cole fervently applied the mechanics of versification in endless variety, although often in haphazard fashion, to describe the external features of nature and to search out their hidden meanings. His poems render faithfully the details of the mountain regions he frequented, and they convey a sense of the wild freedom inherent in the American landscape.

Poetry was but one of Cole's talents. This volume of his poetry is intended to complement other works which *together* provide an insight into Cole and his times. Essential reading is the biography titled THE LIFE AND WORKS OF THOMAS COLE written by Cole's friend Louis L. Noble and published in 1853 (see footnote 13). For visual materials see Howard S. Merritt's catalogue THOMAS COLE prepared in conjunction with the exhibit organized by the Memorial Art Gallery of the University of Rochester in 1969. Two additional major research endeavors are presently being conducted, one by David C. Huntington and the other by Howard S. Merritt. Publication of their findings and wider exposure of Cole's journals will augment existing works.

Thomas Cole needs to be recognized in American literary history as a minor but authentic voice for a generation of artists and writers who were eager to extol the resources of our virgin continent.

REFERENCES

1. Nathan, Walter L. (1961) "Thomas Cole and the Romantic Landscape" in George Boss, ed., ROMANTICISM IN AMERICA: Baltimore, pp. 33-34.

2. McCoubrey, John W. (1965) AMERICAN ART 1700-1960: SOURCES AND DOCUMENTS: Englewood Cliffs, pp. 101-102. All subsequent quotations from Cole's essay, originally published in THE AMERICAN MONTHLY MAGAZINE, I (January, 1836), are taken from this source.

3. Gerdts, William H., Jr. (1967) "Cole's Painting: *After the Temptation*" in STUDIES ON THOMAS COLE, AN AMERICAN ROMANTICIST: Baltimore Museum of Art ANNUAL II, p. 106.
   See paintings *Mountain Sunrise* (1826), *View near Ticonderoga* (1826) and *John the Baptist Preaching in the Wilderness* (1827) for specific examples of this technique.

4. Nash, Roderick (1967) WILDERNESS AND THE AMERICAN MIND: New Haven, p. 79.

5. Poem 16 on page 59.

6. McCoubrey, p. 107.

7. McCoubrey, p. 103.

8. McCoubrey, p. 107.

9. Gerdts, p. 106.

10. McCoubrey, p. 99.

11. I am indebted to Kenneth J. LaBudde's study of the moral and religious themes in Cole's poetry and paintings.

12. Ringe, Donald A. (1954) "Kindred Spirits: Bryant and Cole" in AMERICAN QUARTERLY, VI, p. 239.

13. Noble, Louis L. (1853) THE LIFE AND WORKS OF THOMAS COLE: New York (edited by Elliott S. Vesell: Cambridge, Mass., 1964), p. 229.

14. Richardson, Edgar P. (1956) "The Romantic Genius of Thomas Cole" in ART NEWS, LV, p. 43.

15. Richardson, Edgar P. (1956) PAINTING IN AMERICA: THE STORY OF 450 YEARS: New York, p. 186.

16. See for example "Complaint of the Forest," page 100, "Winds," page 131, "Mt. Etna," page 134, and "The Voyage of Life," page 145.

17. Bryant, William Cullen (1848) A FUNERAL ORATION OCCASIONED BY THE DEATH OF THOMAS COLE: New York, p. 14.

A NOTE ON THE COLE MANUSCRIPTS

The New York State Library in Albany has the largest collection of Cole papers, which includes his essays, sketches, letters, journals, and the majority of the poetry. Additional poems are in the Research Library of the Detroit Institute of Arts.

Most of the poems are in rough draft form. Although the manuscripts are filled with textural annotations, Cole did not, in most instances, re-copy or revise his work. He wrote on assorted scraps of paper, backsides of budget sheets, and sales receipts. Several poems are written on the back of announcements of his *Voyage of Life* series, while others were scribbled on flyers for his *Falls of Niagara* exhibition of 1838. Some poems are scattered throughout his sketchbooks and journals which he kept from 1834-1848. Only a handful are neatly copied onto separate sheets of stationery. Actually, the only tidy record Cole kept of his work is a partially completed verse notebook dated 1825.

Many of the poems are so badly faded or were so hastily penned that it is difficult to decipher the handwriting. At least half of the manuscript pages are undated loose sheets, which makes it impossible to arrange them chronologically.

A CHRONOLOGY OF THE LIFE, PRINCIPAL WORKS AND PUBLISHED WRITINGS OF THOMAS COLE

1801   Born February 1 at Bolton-le-Moor, Lancashire, England.

1818[1]   Cole family temporarily settles in Philadelphia.

1820   Trip to St. Eustatia, West Indies; joins family in Steubenville, Ohio.

1821-   Designs patterns in father's wallpaper shop; works as wood en-
1823   graver; first exposure to craft of painting from itinerant portrait painter, Stein; tries hand at portrait painting.

1823   Moves to Philadelphia, where he studies at Pennsylvania Academy of Fine Arts.

1825   Joins family in New York; opens studio; first sketching trip up the Hudson River; *Falls of the Kaaterskill, View of Fort Putnam* and *Lake with Dead Trees,* which are purchased by William Dunlap, Asher Durand and Jonathan Trumbull; "Emma Moreton, a West Indian Tale," published in THE SATURDAY EVENING POST.

1826   Elected to the National Academy of Design; Robert Gilmore, a Baltimore merchant and art collector, becomes a patron.

1827   First summer in Catskill Mountains where he begins to sketch and write in his nature journal, "Catskilliana"; completes scene from *The Last of the Mohicans;* Daniel Wadsworth, a Hartford merchant and founder in 1844 of the Wadsworth Atheneum Gallery, becomes a patron.

1828   *The Garden of Eden* and *The Expulsion from the Garden of Eden* exhibited at National Academy of Design.

1829-   First European trip; exhibits at British Gallery and Royal
1832   Academy; studies art works at Florence, Rome; exhibits *Sunset on the Arno* at Academy of St. Luke, Florence; *A Wild Scene* painted for Gilmore.

1833   Luman Reed, influential art patron, commissions *The Course of Empire.*

---

1 Louis Noble gives a date of 1819. Later sources mention 1818.

1834   *The Titan's Goblet* exhibited at National Academy of Design.

1835   Reads "Essay on American Scenery" at New York Lyceum; *A Tornado* completed.

1836   Completes *The Course of Empire;* paints *The Oxbow* as exhibition entry for National Academy of Design annual; "Essay on American Scenery" published in THE AMERICAN MONTHLY MAGAZINE; marries Maria Bartow and establishes a permanent home at Catskill, N. Y.

1837   *The Departure* and *The Return* painted for W. P. Van Rensselaer.

1838   *Schroon Mountain, Dreams of Arcadia, The Past* and *The Present.*

1839   Begins *The Voyage of Life* for Samuel Ward.

1840   *Voyage of Life* and *The Architect's Dream* exhibited at National Academy of Design; a poem, "The Summer Days Are Ended," and "A Letter to Critics on the Art of Painting" published in THE KNICKERBOCKER.

1841   Two poems, "The Lament of the Forest" and "Winds," published in THE KNICKERBOCKER; "Lecture Delivered before the Catskill Lyceum on April 1, 1841" published in THE NORTHERN LIGHT.

1841- Second European trip; visits London, Paris, Rome, Sicily; paints
1842   second set of *The Voyage of Life.*

1843   *Angels Administering to Christ in the Wilderness.*

1844   Takes first pupil, Frederick Edwin Church; "Sicilian Scenery and Antiquities" published in THE KNICKERBOCKER.

1845   *L'Allegro* and *Il Penseroso.*

1846   Begins *The Cross and the World,* his largest series, left unfinished at his death; "Letter about Frescoes" published in THE CHURCHMAN.

1847   *Prometheus Bound* exhibited in London.

1848   Dies at Catskill, February 11.

....

1848   American Art Union Memorial Exhibition.

1853   Louis L. Noble's biography published.

POEMS

1

The Times

The Times in this old beldame[1] earth,
Of trial, trouble, and vexation;
Have been the subject, and the birth;
Of many a tiresome conversation.

When I was young the times were bad;
And desp'rate bad each person says:
(And oft I heard that cry so sad)
That money's money now a days.

When I was more observant grown
(I think I heard somebody say)
Such times as these were never known
And money's money every day.

Now I am older; grown more wise;
And things yet keep in their old ways,
This Truth I think around us flies;
There is no money now a days.

                              Steubenville
                              1819

2.

Fancy

How vainly weak is language to express
Th' harmonious beauty of her heavenly song
The azure brightness of the summer sky
As true as pictur'd on the muddy stream
As are the soul-enchanting lays I heard
Told by my feeble[1] tongue to mortal ears —
"O Why," I cried — "thou wand'ring bashful Maid
Fliest thou to wilds and solitudes like these
Come with me come to the cheerful haunts of men
And breath to them thy rich delighting strains."
"No," she replied, "no list'ning ear but thine
Will think my voice my harp's wild notes are sweet
Amidst the din of the tumultuous world
My loudest voice would rise unheard, unknown,
And with my sweetest notes foul Criticism
Might join its fiendish screech. And Envy's breath
Might change each string upon my Silver Harp
To hideous snakes hissing strange discord —
O tempt me not to seek the praise of men
But rather stray with me through Nature's wilds
Thou lov'st me as thy life then wherefore risk
Thy happiness. E'en from thy life's first dawn
Until this hour have we not partners been
Through joy and grief. And I will bless thee still
Thou over arid plains thou wind thy way
Oer flinty paths and barren wilderness
Still to my magic touch the flow'rs shall spring
And spread a carpet for thy weary feet —
The blackest mountain I will gild for thee
And light the ocean in the darkest night
Where'er thou strayest I will cheer thy path
And with my voice will bless thy loveliest hour
Yes while thy spirit wanders upon earth

With thee unceasing dwell for am I not
Thine own thy long lov'd dearly cherish'd Fancy."

Thomas Cole
1825

3

The Vision of Life

High on the swift and stayless wing of Time
Traversing free infinity's dim space
For years I slept and dreamed; but one day called
By some mysterious spirit I awoke —
Thus spoke the voice: "Rouse thee and look around
What dost thou see — *below* — *before* — *behind?*"
I rose unwillingly from my place of rest
And looked *below* — it was a desolate scene
That met my eye — Bare rocks and rugged hills
And black pools and furious cataracts —
Castles there were tattering in ruin
Gardens laid out with the intent to beauty;
But left unfinished, and nought but weeds
And plants pale in the poisoned sickliness
Could vegetate in that accursed soil —
From the drear scene I turned in pain away
And looked *before:* there shadowy fogs were spread
And a black night was brooding o'er the land;
But through the gloom an *ignus fatuus*[1] sped
And threw its light in fitful flickerings,
On any forms that sprung as if from Chaos,
Ever changeful; and at times they took bright forms
As palaces of clustered gems and gold
That shone in sunny splendor on the clouds
Vast rolling far beneath and fountains pure
Mid quiet groves gushed as with living light —
And e'en the music of their warbling came
Soft on the breeze — Anon some evil power[2]
Those gorgeous scenes transformed,[3] into the dark,
Dank, slimy haunt of serpents and of green dragons —
And then from deep and sulphury caverns burst
The dinful howl of demons ever torturing
And forever tortured — "Spirit," I cried:
"Let me not gaze on such soul sickening sights

As these" — "Turn then *behind* thy wearied eye."
Eager I gazed — What heavenly scenes were there!
Over the rocks, the rugged barren hills,
The deep black pools, the furious cataracts,
Distance had spread a veil of tender beauty;
And the drear, desolate wild, that we had passed —
Retiring grew more lovely ere 'twas lost —
"Is this my destined lot," I sighing said, "thou spirit
Ne'er to find joy, but in the fading past?
Bliss sicklied with regret" — The spirit spoke again
But faint and brokenly: and much escaped
My lingering ear — "another state of being"
"Eternity" — "good, evil" — "woe and bliss"
Were all I gathered more.

1825

4.

To the Moon

Hail thou fair orb! Thou ever beauteous light
Thou di'mond in the subtle robe of night
Plac'd by thy maker in the wilds of space,
And bade pursue unceasingly thy race.
In heav'n's blue canopy thy torch was hung
(When the bright angels first creation sung.)
To cheer this earth when in the Ocean's breast
The wearied sun hath plunged his golden crest —

Emblem of mercy: whose descending beams
Impartial spread wide o'er the trackless wild
The fertile valley, and the sparkling deep
The palace, cot, the wood entangled steep.

O what a subject, what a swelling theme
For mind's wide scope, or fancy's airy dream,
To trace enamoured on thy bosom bright,
The rising mountains, or the ocean's light —

Thou hast thy hills rejoicing in the day
Thy rivers roll their ever changeful way.
High to the sun thy threat'ning rocks arise:
And vallies dim my eager fancy spies:
Thy woods are dark — and shall I venture more,
And dare thy hidden secrets to explore;
Are there not beings form'd to grace the rest
Happy, and beautiful, divinely bless'd
Pure as their skies more virtuous than we;
Who never fell from heaven's high destiny —
On the Atlantic's undulating breast,
Thy pictur'd image by the flood is press'd;
Methinks thy searching beams can sweep
Into the very caverns of the deep —
Through liquid mazes troublous, and dread,

Lighting the gloom of Ocean's rocky bed.
Perhaps in some coral grove, or weedy vale
To her he loves the Merman breathes his tale;
In liquid language he recites it o'er,
With voice like waves upon the pebbly shore
Swears that his love is boundless as the sea,
Pure as that orb, and turning points to thee —

O let me wander in my silent beam,
When all is calm, and still, and e'en the stream
Rolls on in silence: when the breezes sleep
Or sigh in softness o'er the smiling deep —

And ye deep woods rise to this silver light,
Heave your broad bosoms toss your branches bright.
And ye blue mountains climbing to the sky
Thou ocean wide: ye beaming clouds on high;
The Moon's fair light in bright reflections raise
And greet the heav'ns with your grateful praise,
Thou light of heaven; who of thee can sing,
Render thy praise, or worthy off'rings bring:
Feeble my efforts but do thou receive,
This humble tribute glorious Queen of eve —

                    T Cole
                    1825

5.

Twilight

The woods are dark; but yet the lingering light
Spreads its last beauty o'er the sunset sky.
How lovely are the portals of the night
When stars come forth to watch the daylight die!

The woods are dark; but yet yon little bird
Is warbling by his newly furnished nest.
No sound beside in all the vale is heard;
But he for rapture cannot — cannot rest.

[1825] [1]

6.

The night was calm. Clad in her mantle darkness
Nature rested. Through Contemplation's Courts
Ubiquitous: unconsciously I stray'd
The free thoughts came: the quickly attending Nymphs
Through the uncounted gates of her vast Halls
Into my presence told their tales and vanish'd;
One form rose more welcome than the rest:
Long had I lov'd and sought th' bewitching Maid —
Like the light mist call'd by the rising sun
To stretch its wreathy pinions and to mount
In exaultation o'er the sluggish world;
To spread its silver hair and to toss
Its snowy arms in the Cerulean [1] Wilds,
The poet's eye may gaze in ecstacy
And Beauty's pow'r may kindle up his heart,
But never can his feeble pen pourtray
The changeful contour of the fleeting Cloud —

So rose the Nymph before my raptur'd eye,
In all her beauty undefinable —
To me she spoke but not as mortals speak;
Words are their signs few they are and pow'rless
But from her lips flow'd Ideas clear and full;
And when her silver Harp she took and sung
And touch'd those strings tun'd in the Choir of Heaven
Each swelling Note rung through my echoing heart —
She sweetly smiled and had me follow her
Into a forest's shade more dark and still
Than the deep cave where single silence dwells —
Here her clear voice pour'd a melodious lay [2]
Harmonious, solemn, and majestic;
The list'ning trees bent through the murky gloom
And wav'd their branches to the pow'rful song.
And when she ceas'd, answering voices came

Loud at first they were but fainter sank,
Then softly whisper'd as from tree to tree
They wandered as unwilling to depart
From these retir'd umbrageous retreats —

Now from the groves we hied and soon I saw
The idle River slowly roll along,
And on its gentle glassy surface dwelt
Reflected objects beautifully soft
E'en the little stars that spring like flow'rs,
Gaily deck the distant fields of Heav'n,
Did twinkle there as bright as in the sky —
And when the mellow notes reach'd the flood
How the waters smil'd and bore their burthen
To the farthest shore —
Now to the deep and narrow vale we sped,
Cleft by some earthquake in the mountain's side
From the deep Chasm the mossy wall arose
And nodding rocks bent o'er the yawning gulf
And form'd an Arch from whose gray central stone
Countless greedy years had suck'd the strength away.
And now it hung suspended o'er the depth.
In dreadful poise like to a little world
Swung by a thread to utmost tension stretch'd
Through the black womb of unencompass'd space —

In murmuring sounds she first began
And the soft music kiss'd in wanton glee
The bare shapeless rocks and in the cliffs
Worn by the trickling stream they playful lurk'd
And mocking lisp'd and lisp'd again again —
But now the voice arose in louder swells
The rude rock trembled and the little fragments
Drop't from the steeps yet, and yet, it mounted
A mighty crash was heard and the huge Arch
That tow'r'd so high lay crumbled at my feet —
Now up a mountain's dangerous steep we sprung
With mountain speed as swift as though we strode

40

Upon the rushing blast that flew tow'rds Heav'n,
The mountain's airy summit soon we gain'd
And stood unwearied on its topmost cliff —
Around us spread a rich and varied feast
For the unsated eye — Over our heads
The Heav'ns' blue Curtain hung without a cloud
Faint and far off upon the reckless Wave
The dim horizon lay — The emblem fit
Of vague Futurity. So far we see
But all beyond is darkness doubt and fear —
On the Ocean's breast numerous islands lay
Like gems upon an azure banner spread
Nearer the dark brown woods, wav'd to the sky
And mighty Streams grasp'd in their Giant arms
The prostrate Earth — There the beauteous Nymph
Rais'd high her Harp and called the slumb'ring Winds
Th' attentive Breezes heard wak'd from their sleep
And sigh'd in softness o'er the sparkling flood
Augmenting. Soon a noisy blast began
To whistle rudely round the mountain top
The tall grass bound before the rushing wind
Hiding their heads the flowers stoop'd for shelter
The careless gale caught up the Maiden's hair
And swept it rudely o'er the troubled strings —
To the blue Heav'ns' interminable voids
Her glitt'ring Harp in silence mute she raised
Tow'rds the Abyss where formless Nothing dwells
Where echoes never lisp though Angels shout —
Again the slumb'ring notes were roused up
As o'er the clear Concave she swung the Harp
Millions! Millions! of stars did smile in light
And shone upon the wand'ring Instrument.
But when the deep red Shield of bloody Mars
Approach'd its edge oft from his fiery eye
She snatch'd it quick. To him she never sung
For he presides o'er gushing Blood and War —
But oft she wept in silence as she mus'd
The Soldier's fall and saw his Glory's Plume

Dyed in his own warm gushing precious blood —
And heard the Widow sigh in loneliness
The Orphan's wail in the Winter's blast
They rais'd their cry bereav'd and unprotected,
For in the field of War their sire was slain;
And cruel grief had rent their Mother's heart
And set her spirit free to rise to Heav'n —
In chasing streams I saw the Maiden's tears
Dash'd on the rocks like broken diamonds.

She rais'd her head, but still a lucent drop
Clung to her long eyelash as though it fear'd
To venture from its lov'd and secret Cell —
A rosy blush now sped across her cheek
And Lo! I saw betwixt the trembling Strings
Fair Venus beam'd! and in enrapturing lays
Were Love and Beauty sung; first Beauty blaz'd
Then lit the torch of Love. The Music's pow'r
Pour'd a rich stream which circles round my heart
And rising fill'd the cistern of my soul
Up to the brim. A nectar'd flood of bliss —
Nor did the Nymph forget that bounteous Queen
Who walks refulgent [3] through the Court of Night
And smiles impartial o'er the trackless wild
The fertile valley and the trem'lous wave
Who from the radiant Crescent on her brow
On all our Wanderings shed a cheering ray —
The sounding Harp was full, and ev'ry string
Drunk in the glorious flood of kindling light
Her sweet voice to its utmost compass rose
And rocks and hills and woods and falling streams
Join'd their loud echoes to th' aspiring song.
From Heav'n she turned from Earth she rais'd her eye
And gaz'd on me while smiles hung round her lips
She thus addressed —

Thou art like the young breeze of the morn
O'er the hills and the valeys it stray'd

On a gay heedless pinion 'twas borne
And it recked [4] not where'er it was laid —
Round the rough Mountain's brow it did play.
And far over the Ocean's blue breast
Through the Meadows of green held its way
And the full blushing Rose it carress'd
But what could it gather or bear
From the rough mountain's brow or the deep
Were not both of them barren and bare
There was nought that the soft breeze could reap
It is true that the grass of the field
Did bow to the breeze as it pass'd
To its kiss the rose blushing did yield
'Twas a perishing Odour at last —
But what of the grass or the rose
Could it carry away in its breast
Again they were left to repose
As though they had never been press'd.
Though beautiful objects it met
Their treasury it never could seize
And 'tis carelessly wandering yet.

1825

7.

For an Album

The voice of Winter in this howling blast
Tells of his quick approach — His chilling breath
Has from the shivering groves their covering cast
And ruthless torn it strews the burthened heath —

But O may wintry time be slow to tear
This Album's richly varied leaves away,
The buds of genius that may blossom there,
And wit's wild flowers innocently gay.

If here the rose of love should chance to blush
Or friendship's foliage tenderly entwine
O may no icy hand the flow'ret crush
Or rudely break the tendrils of the vine —

And may thy life fair Delia[1] softly flow
A gentle stream through fields of joy its way
Untroubled by the bitter storms of war
Unclouded as a beauteous summer's day —

November, 1826

8.

Lines on Lake George[1]

Awake! The fresh morn breaks the mountains grey
From the dark pillow of the gloomy night
Reanimated raise their heads; Awake!
Before thee lies the Holy Lake outspread,
The blue Horican[2] with its countless isles:
Yet are the mists shadowing its bosom.
Wake!
On all the varied bosom of this earth
This is the truest mirror of the sky
And the fair moon as oft she rises o'er
The eastern mountain's summit lingers there
Enamoured: no earthly wave beside
Returns her silver brightness to the skies,
Unmingled with its own dark turbidness;
The stars are pictured here so faithfully,
That the lone wanderer on its pebbly shore,
Doubts his own vision and with caution treads
Upon the margin of the lower sky —

The sun is smiling on yon distant isles
That hang so tremulously o'er the deep —
Nature in frolic once stretch'd forth her hand
And from her mine of glittering gems conveyed
Some glowing emeralds and careless o'er
A crystal tablet strew'd them. There they lie
In fragments spread, broken, — but beautiful —

And yet how bright, how tranquil, how unearthly,
How clear the bosom of this silver lake —
Pleased with the privilege the eye explores
The wat'ry realms and sees o'er golden sands
The scaly thousands playing; the tall pine
That shaded once the topmost cliff now resting

Within some nook, as in a sepulchre,
Wrap'd in a winding sheet of moss and weeds —
O! that men's hearts were open as this wave
Unto man's gazing and were found as spotless —
Well might the holy priest crave for the fount[3]
So pure a stream; and doubly blessed were they,
Who felt the sacred cross mark'd on their brows,
In the cool impress of the saving flood —

Not always was it pure as now 'tis seen
The streams that pay their tribute to the lake,
Were crimson'd once by men's hot blood, and cast
Upon the waters blue, their horrid stain —
But it has purified itself long since:
The ruddy blush of shame but briefly dwells
Upon the open brow of innocence —

Yes! in yon narrow defile shut from day —
Where doves now coo beneath the shade unsear'd;
The warriors met thrice times in one short day —

There is a rock now resting in that glen
That could it speak of chivalrous deeds 'twould tell
How the warm heart's blood trickled through the moss
That covers it, how the stern warrior
Faint with the loss of blood grasp'd its grey top
Frowned on his enemy and fell, and died —

Of that relentless massacre[4] yon hills
Were witness, they echo'd back the groans
Of unarmed warriors, dying female shrieks,
And the weak plaint of feeble innocence;
Mingled with yells of Indians banqueting
In blood —

Turn from those sickening scenes of horror turn,
Who that can gaze upon that dimpled lake;
Would ever think that o'er its smiling face
The trumpet's voice hath hoarsely sent defiance,

46

That the green shores reflected there have been
The ample stage whereon the bloody tragedy
Of war was acted — one would well suppose
That when men look'd upon its tranquil face
The high tempestuous waves of passion's storm
Would settle into peacefulness — but man
When in his breast rage hatred and revenge,
Heeds not the quiet whisperings of nature —

Happy are these calm and lovely days of peace
The din of war with years hath pass'd away
The trumpets thrilling voice does sometimes wake
The sleeping echoes from their mountain couch
But dying shrieks ne'er mingle with its tones —

O may the voice of music that so chime
With the wild mountain breeze and rippling lake
Ne'er wake the soul but to a keener sense
Of nature's beauties — How reluctant I
Leave thy bright shores thou lov'd Horican
But like yon skiff that glides away and melts
In the wild distance — I may journey far
Yet will my mind be dwelling upon thee;
Yet the soft lisping of thy crystal wave
Shall echo in my soul when I am far away.

T. Cole
1826

LANDSCAPE SCENE FROM "THE LAST OF THE MOHICANS"
1827
New York State Historical Association
Cooperstown, New York

9.

To Mount Washington [1]

Hail Monarch of a thousand giant hills!
Who settest proudly on the earth thy throne!
Crowned with the clouds and the lightenings. Hail!
Vast monument of power that God hath reared
Upon the lowly earth to conquer time
And measure out eternity — what sage
So wise can tell when first thy dark rude top
Pierc'd the blue heavens and with the sun midway —
The season — hour — when thou shalt melt away
And vanish like the cloudy mists thou art now nursing?
When the all powerful hand of God shall crush
Thy pond'rous rocks, and cast the dust
Upon the changeful and unresting winds?
Not one: Man's vaunted works since thou wert reared
Have risen and crumbled — oblivious night
Hath blotted empires out. And mighty things
Have perish'd like a breath that only dying lives —

October, 1828 [2]

49

10.

Niagara

Softly the light in these umbrageous realms
Falls on the path, and plays upon the leaf —
Softly the breeze now whispering steals between
The thousand pillars of the quiet wood —
And we with gentle musings, and fond thoughts
Untroubled, free, pursue our pleasant way —

What sound is that careering on the wings
Of stormy blasts, so mightily and fills
The lofty arches of the forest wide?
Is it the clamor of impetuous winds
That strive for egress from some rock-bound cave?
Or is an earthquake waking from its wrath
And from the high unstable mountain tops
Hurling the ponderous and rebounding rocks?

No! tis Niagara shouts from the abyss
Where headlong he has cast him in his might!
And rocks, and woods, and the astounded air,
And earth's deep center tremble as with fear —

Approach and view the wonder of a world
See! when the waters of a hundred lakes
An unheaped multitude tumultuous leap
O'er the projecting crags, into the gulf —

Thence the thick mist perpetual ascends,
In cloudy piles into the sky and hides,
The quivering torment of the floods below —
Like steam emitted from some cauldron vast
Vexed by furious and unquenching fires —

Thou consummation of the earth's sublime!
Thy course nor time, nor tide, nor change hath stemmed!

Thy voice hath risen above the tempest's roar
Year after year till countless they are grown —

    Seasons have looked upon thee and have died —
    Ages have vanish'd and the earth grown old —
    Man who hath moved mountains, bound the sea,
    Awe-struck recoils and works on thee no change -

The earth hath much of beauty but the choice
Is garlanded around thine august brows —
Yon, flaky foam is white as alpine snow —
Yon gushing emerald clear as ocean's depths —
The bow of promise sits on sable clouds;
But lo! a far excelling iris[1] girds
The dazzling splendour of thy snowy breast —

Ages untold thy voice broke forth unheard;
But by the shrinking wolf, or the tim'rous deer
Or wandering savage of the echoing wild —
Until an enterprise sublime unbarred
The mighty portals of the golden west
And midst its teeming fulness thou wast found
Majestic in the wilderness enthroned —

               Written at the Falls[2]
               May, 1829

11.

Alas! he is a wretch who has no home,[1]
Kindred nor friends on whom to turn his thought,
Whose lot is o'er the cold wide world to roam:
Whose season of return is never sought
Whose wanderings are alike unmark'd — unknown
By Mother, Sister, Wife, by any loving one —

He is a torn weed on a desolate sea
Toss'd by the waves and beaten by the winds
And driven by currents unresistingly
From deep to deep, and never finds
A peaceful haven when the tide will[2] fling
It gently round some mossy rock to cling.

And like the wind on some vast wilderness
That sighing seeketh rest, but seeks in vain,
Unlov'd and uncarress'd, companionless
It mournful wanders o'er the dreary plain.
If to outlive affection is my doom
Welcome will be the shelter of the Tomb.

1829

12.

Let not the ostentatious gaud of art,
That tempts the eye, but touches not the heart,
Lure me from nature's purer love divine:
But, like a pilgrim, at some holy shrine,
Bow down to her devotedly, and learn,
In her most sacred features, to discern
That truth is beauty.

[1829][1]

13.

Written on my Birthday, Feb. 1, 1830[1]

Into the deep of the eternal past,
Another year hath sunk and what alas?
Is saved from the wreck, but recollections dim
Of unripe joys, and fears and hopes vague
And evanescent as the morning mists —

Another year is past! Where are the joys
That hope had wreathed round the year like flowers,
Last Natal day? Lov'd shadows they are fled —

O fickle Fortune — as the rainbow deck'd,
Like it forever flying when pursued,
Unjust. How oft into the lap of sloth
Thy treasures rich are cast — And thou bright Fame,[2]
Through bitter storms hath led; and in the night
When wearied nature has demanded sleep
Hath waked me up to gaze on thee. How cold
Thy beams! How distant is thy sphere!
Did ever lover with so chaste a flame
And so devoted meet with such ill success —

Ye children of my fancy and my care!
Neglected and despised and careless cast
Into the shade,[3] unmark'd amid the crowd[4]
That have a name; or gaudy force, the gaze
And wonder of the ignorant and vain —
Are ye devoid of beauty? Can no eye
Delight in you but mine? perhaps too fond
My fancy pictures scenes and desires
They on the canvas glow and live, where naught
But formal insipidity exists —

How oft the voice of praise breaks forth o'er works
More fortunate than mine and there descants

How skillfully the orb hath mimick'd nature
How every tent and form is beautiful and true —
Then pass me by as though I ne'er had drank
One draught at the great universal spring —
Ye mountains, woods, rocks, and impetuous streams
Ye mantling heav'ns — Speak — speak for me!
Have I not held communion close with you
And like to one who is enamoured, gazed
Intensely on your ever varying charms,
And has it been in vain?

14.

Written on my Birthday, Feb. 1, 1830

Into the deep of the eternal past
Another year is sunk and what alas!
Is saved from the wreck, but recollections dim
Of unripe joys, of fears and hopes as vague
And evanescent as the morning mists.

Another year is past, where are the joys
Hope had enwreathed around the year like flowers
Last Natal day? Loved shadows they are fled.
O fickle Fortune — as the rainbow decked
Like it, forever flying when pursued.
Unjust! How oft into the lap of Sloth
Thy treasures rich are cast. And thou bright Fame,
The star that o'er the mountains and the sea
Through beating storms have led me, and at night
When wearied nature has demanded sleep
Hath waked me up to gaze on thee — How cold
Thy glittering beams! How distant is thy sphere!
Did ever lover with so chaste a flame,
And so devoted, meet such ill success.

Ye children of my fancy and my care
Neglected and despised and careless cast
Into the shade unmarked amid the crowd
That have a name, or gaudy, force the gaze
And wonder of the ignorant and light;
Are ye devoid of beauty? Can no eye
Delight in you but mine. Ah perhaps too fond
My fancy pictures gorgeous scenes and desires
They on the canvas glow and live where nought
But labored insipidity exists.

How oft the voice of praise breaks o'er work,
More fortunate than mine and there descants

How skilfully the art hath mimicked nature
How every tent and form is beautiful and true,
Then pass me by as though I ne'er had drunk
One draught at the great universal spring —

Ye mountains, woods and rocky, impetuous streams
Ye wide spread heavens! Speak O speak for me!
Have I not held communion close with you
And like to one who is enamoured, gazed
Intensely on your ever varying charms;
And has it been in vain?

15.

I see the green Fiesole[1] arise,
A pyramid whose flowers and vine-clad steeps,
Are proudly crown'd by ancient walls, where lies
The latest loveliest sunbeam when it sleeps
To shade and Arno[2] winding through the vale,
Grows brighter as the shades of earth prevail —
Fiesole and Arno both are fam'd in song[3]
I view your beauty; but I cannot feel;
And grieve to find my heart can do me wrong.
There is a blight on me, a stoney chill —
Upon the glow of heaven and earth I gaze,
But do not burn as in my earlier days —

O let me leave the world if it can steal
Nature's best dower from me — the gift to feel.

Florence
June, 1831

16.

A lonely cloud is flitting round the brow
Of the dark barren mountain; but the glow
Of the unrisen sun illumes each fold
Transmuting blackness into living gold —
And so around my des'late soul does cling
One melancholy thought — a shadowy thing
Which from the world has sprung, in a dark hour
When the worst genius of my fate had power —
But hope is dawning — and its sun will rise
From death's deep ocean, and the distant skies
Already cast a tone delightful o'er my mind
And to my sojourn here shall make resign'd.
For Time will quickly waft me o'er that sea
When earthly sorrow cannot follow me.[1]

Catskill
1832

17.[1]

The eager vessel flies the broken surge,
The surge that it has broken — so my soul
Leaving the stormy past does onward urge
Its course through the wild waves that roll
Tempestuously — The sea-worn bark
Strained by a thousand storms; heeds not the helm
But aimless plunges through the uncertain dark —
Around are rocks and shoals, a horrid realm!
Thou guardian spirit — whom a mother's prayer
Brought down from heaven to guard her son,
Be watchful — shield and protect from snares
Of sin — And let the haven soon be won —
The welcome home of everlasting peace
Where pain and trouble shall forever cease.

Catskill
1832

18.

The eager vessel flies the broken surge,
The surge which it has broken — so my soul
Leaving the stormy past does onward urge
Its course through the wild waves of life that roll
Tempestuously — The sea-worn bark
Strained by a thousand storms[1] heeds not the helm
But aimless plunges through the uncertain dark —
Around are rocks and shoals, a horrid realm!
    Thou guardian Spirit! whom a mother's prayer
    Brought down from heaven to guard her son
    Be watchful — protect him from the snares
    Of sin — and let the haven soon be won
    The welcome home of everlasting peace
    When rocks ne'er threaten and the tempests cease.

                  Catskill
                  1834

19.

Lines Written after a Walk on [a] Beautiful Morning in November —[1]

Unhoped for joys are always welcomest,
And fountains in the desert doubly bless'd —
So 'mid the storms of the declining year
More beautiful the sunny hours appear —
From darkling dreams of night I wake, and lo!
Through the unmeasured depths of heaven flow,
The unresounding tides of gold and azure —
The earth with light is filled, my heart with pleasure.

My footsteps lead through that contiguous grove,
Where oft I've wander'd with the friends I love;
But 'tis no more umbrageous and green
As in the summer months; but slant between
The innumerable trunks the sunbeams play,
And weave with shade, a mingled night and day.
Hid is the earth, by withering foliage brown'd
The brightest loveliest wild-flowers' chosen ground;
Where beamed amid the shade their modest eyes,
The walnut now and chaliced acorn lies —
Crush'd are the crackling leaves although I tread
Gently; for I remember o'er my head,
In July's sultriness and glare they made
A most inviting paradise of shade;
Coolness and perfume giving to the breeze,
And to the soul an atmosphere of peace —
O! never! never! should the friends laid low,
(Like these sere leaves) from out the memory go;
And as around their graves we chance to tread,
Let us recall the virtues of the dead —
For even these relics of the vanish'd year
A lingering, living, balmy fragrance bear —

The Hudson lies below, a mirror'd heaven;
Stainless, save where the joyous hills are given
With grassy slope, dark rock, and breezy wood
In purple beauty to the wooing flood —
Yon sails unruffled now, by torturing storms,
Like swans enamoured of their own bright forms;
Or spirits that have left the sky to gaze
Upon the earth's clear mirror, in amaze —
Supported on unclosing wings they float
As wind-borne music's softest, sweetest note.
But yet they move, the deep unresting tide
Bears quickly onward; distance soon will hide
Their voyaging towards the main — Thus we
Upon the winding stream of human life,
In its calm, happier days, when wo and strife
Are far; live all within ourselves — forget
The ebbing tide of time, is swiftly set
Towards eternity; nor think that storm
May soon o'ertake us, and our course deform —
E'en now upon yon distant bark a change
Is come — the west-wind in its boundless range
Has breathed upon it gently, and a shade
Deep blue and dark of rippling waves is laid
Athwart the lower heaven and from the stream
The pictured form is vanish'd like a dream —

The mountains are before me; the strong chain
That binds to central earth the prostrate plain —
They like high watch-towers o'er the wide spread land
Upon the shore of heaven's ocean stand —
And I have thought that such might landmarks be
To voyaging spirits on th' etherial sea —
And they are still; and stern — with fixed look;
But beautiful like those who have forsook
All earthly thoughts for holier things on high
And hold alone communion with the sky —

Few days are past, since in a robe of gold,
And purple they were clad; but now the fold,

Is of a soberer hue and thinly spread
Like drapery o'er the features of the dead —
From those aerial castles to my feet
Extends a scene such as the eye can meet
Not frequently, although earth's realms are wide
And beauty does in every clime abide —
A landscape where, lawn, wood so interlace
And hill meets vale in such a soft embrace;
And in the midst a basin deeply placed
To catch the azure that the heavens waste —
Poets may leave their Grecian Temple well
Content, in this our western vale to dwell.

I hear the voice of stillness the sweet sound
Of unseen waters, that from some profound
Have utt'rance, filling the echoless sky
With one long breath of music — And the sigh
Of the responsive hills, is like soft grief
That in itself alone, finds best relief —

O! let me fill my soul with this bright scene
And garner up its beauty ere the sheen
That this heaven-favored day has given,
By wintry storms is from its bosom riven —
Though now it glows resplendent 'neath the sun;
And streams through silent groves undimpled run;
And mountain shades alone in hollows lie,
Those calm blue cradles of tranquility —
And the unrobed woods are softly warm
And quiet sleeping as though never storm
Had tortured them — Alas! too soon must come
The conflict of the winds, that from the womb,
Of the vast circumambient shall be born
Giants — He of the south who howls in scorn,
And heaves the deluge on the shrinking land —
And He who from the north puts forth his hand,
And shakes down heaven in the chilling drift,
And wields the viewless ice-bolt keen and swift —
E'en now upon the far horizons verge

A gloom uplifts; it is the foremost surge,
Of winter's darksome sea —

                    So quickly fly
All beauteous things, we gaze and love — they die.
Be it not mine ungrateful thoughts to raise;
Beauty though transient, sheds on us its rays,
To warm and vivifie — Transient is the sun;
But earth rejoices as his course is run —

                              T. C.
                              Catskill
                              1833

20.

Vain is my fondest hope! Alone — alone
Through the wide weary world, I tread nor find
That loving spirit — that congenial one,
Would mingle soul with my soul — mind with mind,
And like two fountains forming one deep stream
Whose waters clear should be divided never;
Warbling their way as beauteous as a dream
Of Heaven, that shall be dreamed and dreamed forever.
Yes! I have wished for one to dream with me
When was my mood the real world to leave
For the far brighter realm of fantasy —
And when descended into earthly care
As clouds must sometimes rest on mountain tops
My sorrows disappointments love to share
And let her joys be my joys — hopes my hopes —
And thus the river of our love should be
Augmenting as it flowed towards Eternity —

1833

21.

On seeing that a favorite tree
of the Author's had been cut down —

And is the glory of the forest dead?
Struck down? Its beauteous foliage spread
On the base earth? O! ruthless was the deed
Destroying man! What demon urg'd the speed
Of thine unpitying axe? Didst thou not know
My heart was wounded by each savage blow?
Could not the lovliness that did begird
These boughs disarm thine hand and save the bird
Its ancient home and me a lasting joy!
Vain is my plaint! All that I love must die.
But death sometimes leaves hope — friends may yet meet
And life be fed on expectation sweet —
But here no hope survives; again shall spread o'er me
Never the gentle shade of my beloved tree —

Catskill
June 22, 1834

22.

On seeing that a favorite tree
of the Author's had been cut down —

And is the glory of the forest dead,
Struck down? — Its beauteous foliage spread
On the base earth? — O! ruthless was the deed
Destroying man! What demon urg'd the speed
Of thine unpitying axe? Didst thou not know
My heart was wounded by each savage blow?
Could not the lovliness that did begird
These boughs, dis-arm thine hand and save the bird
Its ancient home, and me a lasting joy? —
Vain is my plaint! All that I love must die;
But death sometimes leaves hope — friends yet may
    meet,
And life be fed on expectation sweet —
But here no hope survives — never again shall o'er me
    spread
Never again, the gentle shade of my beloved tree —

                              Catskill
                              June 22, 1834

68

23.

The Painter's Lamentation[1]

That there should be a poison in sweet looks
Alas! — Alas that all the tameless brooks
Which murmur wildly through the vale of love
Should taste of bitterness! That those who rove
The labarynthine dell, should go astray
Bewildered, blinded, heedless of the way
Of wisdom and of peace! — Such is my fate —
And O ye mountains that I lov'd of late
My early adoration yet despite not him,
Who now though not forgetting doth neglect
Your charms — Sighing he owns the deep defect;
But destiny unkind and unexpected care,
Have torn him from you, and a fond despair
Embraces now his heart and in its core
Is rooted deep and perhaps forever more —

Thou radiant spirit! whose dear controul
Long time hath bless'd me — Sister of my soul!
And wonder of all eyes! My glorious art!
Wilt thou desert and desolate the heart
Which thou hast shielded through so many years
From various ills? — Then have I cause for tears —
For from my sweet lips I have drunk the dew
Of more than earthly happiness, and drew
From out thy taintless breath etherial joy —
An essence heavenly — alas that it should die —

And this because a mortal feeling came —
A gush as of unconquerable flame
Consumes my heart — But this is vain —
I am the guilty and why do I complain? —
Because my crime is one I cannot hate —
Because it is a shadow which my fate
Cast over me — It like a cloud arose,
Gently and beautifully — budded like a rose —

I dream'd not such a bright cloud could ere contain,
When first 'twas seen, fierce tempests dark and rain
Or that the bud, so beautiful, in its core
A blackness and a bitter poison bore —

It is no crime to love; but it is pain
To me and torture — for I ne'er shall gain
Her whom I so desire — her heart is cold
But perhaps 'twould melt beneath the touch of gold —
That talisman I have not — nor desire
To kindle ought but love's unsordid fire —
A hour's departed, have ye no return?
Have ye no spring, like flowers? Does then the urn
Of Time contain, nought but unquick'ning dust
Of the past lov'd and beautiful? And must
Our dearest sunniest pleasure pass away
And endless night succeed the swift-wing'd day?

Ah me! I little dream'd when wand'ring free
In heart and mind, in lands beyond the sea —
That 'mid the mountains of my early love,
I should unlearn their beauty, — or more true,
My heart should learn unfaithfulness — The dew
Of morning yet ascends in misty wreaths,
To bind their brows of majesty — the wind yet breathes
Through the dark forests that around them cling,
And on their crags the eagle flaps his wing —

Those were bright hours my loving mem'ry sees,
When by the convent gray I sat — beneath the trees
That shadowy wave on Mont Albana's[2] top,
An emerald crown barbarian time did drop
Relenting that the marble-columned pile
That once stood there his rude hands did despoil.[3]
And Rome was at my feet, but far below,
Its ruined heaps still sparkling in the glow
Of the unfading sun, which shone as bright
As in the conquering Carthaginians' sight — [4]
Around the wide Campagna's[5] waste of green

Lay like a shipless sea — though wrecks were seen
Of duct and tower — many a golden chain
On its breast broken — ne'er to join again —
Sracte[6] like an island shone afar
The sabine[7] mountains made the eastern bar
While on the west — the tideless beauteous sea
Pillowed the plain that slumb'red tranquilly —

But this is past — and my soul's freshness gone
The lyre is broken — the harp has lost its tone —
O babbling stream! That flowest careless on
In everlasting joy! — Where! where is flown
Thy beauty? — How art thou chang'd since last
I stood upon thy margin — has it pass'd
With the quick hours that stole my peace?
I never deem'd thy lovliness would cease
Over the bright rocks yet I see thee skim;
Thou art *not* chang'd stream! — My eyes are dim —

O pride thou yet unconqurable one,
Come to my aid — steel me and let me frown
Instead of weep — break — break the cankering chain
That binds me — let no love remain
To fester in my bosom — let my art
Again, alone, be mistress of my heart —

[July, 1834][8]

24.

Again the wreathed snow
Girdles and crowns the mountains:
Again is chain'd the flow
Of the once joyous fountains:

Again the dark gray forests wildly wave
With doleful music in the biting blast
Unlike the gentle murmurings they gave
When summer's foliage was o'er them cast —

And yet I linger here;
The City calls aloud
To leave the woodlands sere
And join the busy crowd —

I loiter gazing o'er the distant hills
That beauty ne'er deserts though clad
In wintry garb; and tarry by the rills
Whose summer warblings oft have made me glad —

Why do I tarry there?
A holy calm pervades
The rural earth — where men
Assemble there is turmoil; but these shades
Are unto me a solemn sacred place,
Where Envy — malice — pride can never come
Or coming, quickly all that demon race
Languish and die — the wildwood is their tomb —

Catskill
November 1, 1834

25.

O Cedar Grove! whene'er I think to part
From thine all peaceful shades my aching heart
Is like to his who leaves some blessed shore
A weeping exile ne'er to see it more —

Catskill
November, 1834

26.

I sigh not for a stormless clime,[1]
Where drowsy quiet ever dwells,
Where purling waters changeless clime
Through soft and green unwinter'd dells —

For storms bring beauty in their train;
The hills that roar'd beneath the blast
The woods that welter'd in the rain
Rejoice whene'er the tempest's past.

Their faces lifting to the sky
With fresher brightness, richer hue;
As though the blast had brought them joy,
Darkness and rain dropp'd gladness too —

So storms of ill when pass'd away
Leave in our souls serene delight;
The blackness of the stormy day,
Doth make[2] the welcome calm more bright —

January 25, 1835

27.

"Cast off the bands that bind thee now
Each strand is steep'd in pain."
Thus spoke a voice — I made a vow
To break them all — 'twas vain —

Shall man within whose heart's core flows
Affection's burning tide
Chill it with wordliness and close
Its gush in icy pride?

He cannot if he has that spark
Of heaven's fire called love
Quenchless it burns amid the storm
True as the stars above.

May 28, 1835

28

Hope and Trust Spring from the Contemplation of the Works of God

Mine eyes bedimmed with tears I heavenward raised
Called by some Spirit of a better sphere,
And through the universal ether gazed
And marked the golden orbs that did appear
To tremble mid the dark abyss profound;
But yet they faltered not; nor sank; nor swerved
In glory marching their majestic round,
In everlasting harmony preserved.

"Is there cause for tears" the spirit said:
"When all these ponderous worlds are thus sustained
By that invisible hand and gently led
Through the wide fields of heaven; like sheep restrained
From wandering by their shepherd's gentle voice.
Within His hand is held thy soul, thine all;
List! thou wilt hear that Shepherd's loving call.
Is there then cause for tears? Thou shouldst rejoice!"

August 16, 1835

MOSES ON THE MOUNT
Shelburne Museum, Incorporated
Shelburne, Vermont

29.

Evening Thoughts

When Evening in the sky sits calm and pure
And all the fleecy clouds are still and bright
And earth beneath the silent air obscure
Waits for the stars that herald in the night;
All earth-born cares unholy cease to move;
Peace dwells on earth and beauty in the sky —
Then is the spirit melted as with love
And tears spring forth upon the brink of joy.
But whence the shade of sadness o'er us thrown
When thoughts are purest in that quiet hour?
From sense of sin arises that sad tone?
Knowing that we alone feel passion's power,
That touches not the mountain far and lone —
        Or is it that the fading light reminds
        That we are mortal and the latter day
        Steals onward swiftly, like the unseen winds,
        And all our years are clouds that quickly pass away.

                        August 23, 1835

30

Evening Thoughts

When Evening in the sky sits calm and pure
And all the fleecy clouds are still and bright,
And earth beneath the silent air obscure
Waits for the stars that herald in the night;
All cares unholy, earth born, cease to move,
Peace dwells on earth and beauty in the sky.
    Then is the spirit melted as with love
    And tears spring forth upon the brink of joy.
But whence the shade of sadness o'er us thrown
When thoughts are purest in the quiet hour?
From sense of sin arises that sad tone?
Knowing that we alone feel passion's power,
That touches not the mountain far and lone?

    Or is it that the fading light reminds
    That we are mortal and the latter day
    Steals onward swiftly, like the unseen winds
    And all our years are clouds that quickly pass away.

Tho Cole
August 23, 1835

31.

Though time has sadden'd every thought,
And kill'd the fresh and flower-like joy;
Sweet hope and memory have brought
A bliss that lives without alloy.

August 25, 1835[1]

32.

Winter had fled into his northern home —
The voice of waters to my charmed ear
Rose as rejoicing that the spring had come
To bless yon vale to me forever dear —
And with the sound melodious did arise
Upon my soul the sense of former joys,
As though the spirit of departed years
Dwelt in that music soft unmix'd with tears —

But sadness sits upon my heart and spring
Comes not with wonted[1] gladness, pleasantly;
But sorrow, gloom, sit darkly on her wing
And though she smiles — her smiles are not for me;
For sickness lays its withering hand, alas!
On one who loves to watch the early grass
And buds come forth and flowers that gently send
Abroad their fragrance sweet — my kindest friend![2]

Catskill
May 23, 1836

33.

On hearing of the death of Mr. Reed —

It came to me — the word that he was dead —
My Benefactor! To myself I said
It is a dream — I strove to wake, Alas!
The dream if such it is will never pass —

The earth is darker though 'tis summer now,
And heaven does wear a shadow on its brow,
And the deep green of the far waving hills
The once gay flowers, the ever singing rills
Have ta'en a tone of sadness and no more
Unlock the springs of joy; but daily pour
An influence regretful on my soul,
And bid forth tears that I would fain controul.
O cease my tears ye are too soft for grief
Grief such as mine — I would not your relief.

Catskill
June, 1836

34.

Lines occasioned by the death of Mr. Luman Reed[1]

If friendship hath the power to lift the soul
Above the common flight of worldly thought;
Or gratitude t' enkindle pure poetic fire,
This pen would flow with ever living words
By sorrow consecrated to the latest time —
And one unskill'd in verse would rev'rent pay
A tribute to thy memory O Reed,
And place a wreath embalm'd by honest tears
Upon thy tomb to bloom forever there —

For thine is not the ruthless conqueror's claim
A proud renown inscrib'd in blood and wrong
Upon men's hearts with wonder and with fear;
But dwelleth in our memory a living light
To cheer and to illumine and to guide
Us who linger mid the shades of life —

O bright example of superior worth!
Would that the world did turn to such as thee
T' admire and emulate and leave the gaud
The ostentation and the baleful glare.
Of those who mounted in Ambition's Car,
Like pestilential meteors swiftly rush
Through the applauding multitude of men
To dazzle and destroy —

            Thy life of peace
Was like the summer cloud that rose at morn
To grace the earth and as the day advanced
Increas'd in beauty; 'till the setting sun
Wrapp'd it in splendour ere the night was come.
That night alas: came at the hour of noon

When least our charmed eyes expected change;
Change such as this so sudden and so dark —
Our hearts were all rejoicing in fond hope,
Full of expectant joy — not dreaming Death
Stood by with icy hand uprais'd to strike —
He struck! Deep in my breast the blow was felt
And droop'd my spirit — he alas! was gone
My ever honoured friend! I look'd around
The earth was dreary and the sunshine past —
I wake at dawn of day and gaze as wont
Upon the hills uplifted to the clouds;
But a cold shadow broods upon my soul
That should enkindle at the glorious sight.
I wander in the evening's twilight calm
When woods and streams sleep 'neath the sapphire sky;
And then the heavenly spirit of the hour
Would steal into my heart, but that 'tis full
Of a deep dwelling sorrow that upheaves
Like a huge billow on some lonely shore
That swells and breaks in mournful music there.
E'en the strong charm of my all matchless art,
Whose fervent votary I claim to be,
And once did deem no earthly cause could mar
Is powerless now and yields me joy no more —
He who is ta'en away did best sustain,
Encourage in the arduous pursuit,
And truly loving it well knew to give
Essential praise and just, and pointed high
To the steep sun-crown'd hill of Excellence.

Earth is the vestibule of Heaven where
Some erring wander and some meekly wait;
Our friend dwelt with us until Death
Who hath the key, did open unto him
The golden gate and we are left without
To tears and darkness, wond'ring what time
We through that glorious portal shall be led
To see that face benign which now can never change.

Sorrow alone should not usurp the pen;
But it should teem with praise most justly due
Not such vain praise as vulgar tongues bestow
On puffed-up favourites of fortune or of fame;
But that which virtue doth from truth demand.
For the warm heart of him we now lament
Was fix'd in strong integrity and truth,
And candour generosity and taste
Grew sweetly round as may the flowers
About the firm-set oak cling not encumb'ring
But spread with beauty, fragrance and rich fruit —

Let not a Cosmo or Lorenzo fam'd
Firenze's favoured princes all engross
Our admiration; for this western land
Had one munificent as they, less proud;
Who lov'd like them to nurse the growing arts,
But with a purer love and more exalted end;
Who plotted not to tyrannise and rule;
But trod the nobler though less dazzling path
That leads up to the Altar of the public weal —

But he is dead! That thought will rise and praise
Is faltering where 'tis grief o'erwhelmed the soul —
The stream may not be stemm'd so let it flow
It hath the power to purify and Hope
Shall spring from out its waters, onward led
By bright example up to virtue's radiant fame —

Summer is past, but not my grief which chords
With the Autumnal blast through the grove
With mournful cadence, 'neath the waning moon,
Sighs fitfully; as the distracted leaves
Are hurried to and fro in wild unrest —
But the rude gale shall cease and winter drear
Again give place unto the coming spring
And the bare groves shall put their verdure on
Rejoicing that the winter winds are spent;

Which came not to destroy; but to prepare
For fresher beauty, renovated youth —
So shall our souls beneath the icy blasts
Of death and sorrow, shrink, but never die
And the dark desolation of the heart
Be but the germe of joy which shall burst forth
In the perennial sunshine of Immortal life.

Catskill
1836

35.

Song of the Spirit of the Mountain

A glorious privilege it is to wear a Spirit's form
And solitary dwell for aye [1] on this high mountain-peak; [2]
To watch afar beneath my feet the darkly heaving storm
And see its cloudy billows o'er the craggy ramparts break;

    To hear the hurrying blast
    Torment the groaning woods
    O'er precipices cast
    The desolating floods. —
    To mark in wreathèd fire
    The crackling pines expire: —

To list the Earthquake's and the Thunder's voice
Round and beneath my everlasting Throne;
Meanwhile unscathed, untouched I still rejoice
And sing my psalm of gladness all alone.
Through the clear ether that surrounds my home
My keen eyes watch the far, bewildering spheres
Each comet wild that tracked the midnight dome,
Within the deep recesses of my mind appears
For ages past. — Years! They are nought to me!
And centuries on centuries roll by harmlessly.
First to salute the Sun when he breaks through the night
I gaze upon him still when Earth has lost its light.

He loves me e'en when winter's gloom enfolds the world below
And lights my mountain-pinnacle enwreathed with drifted snow
That mid deep heaven lifted high by mortals seen afar
Through rifts of sable clouds appears a new and burning star.

    When silence is most deathlike
    And darkness deepest cast,
    The streamlet's voice is breathlike
    And dews are falling fast;

Far through the azure depths above, my clarion-songs resound;
Like voices of winds and waves and woods and deep tones of
    the ground
I wave my shadeless pinions o'er this my calm domain;
A solitary realm it is; but where 'tis joy to reign.

[July, 1837] [3]

36

The wight[1] who climbs the mountain's gleaming side
Treads not the azure that he saw from far
But rugged rocks and ravines dark and wide: —
And dangerous steeps and precipices mar
The hill's broad sky-ward bosom and the shady dell
Where once, in the distance viewing, he had long'd to
    dwell.

Nor in th' aerial nook, espied on high,
Screen'd from the sun's intensest ray,
The seeming haunt of bless'd tranquility,
He finds repose — There 'mid the deaf'ning bray
Of cataracts, grisly crags and ever dripping rocks,
Forever desolate, the narrow vale enlocks —

It was the heaven stooping to the world,
The crystal ether of supernal space,
That smooth'd the rugged wild and soft unfurled
A veil of beauty o'er the mountain's face —
So bare, dark is human thought till heaven descends
And to its aspect drear celestial beauty lends —

July 14, 1837

37.

Written in Autumn

Another year like a frail flower is bound
In time's sere [1] withering aye [2] to cling,
Eternity, thy shadowy temples round,
Like to the musick of a broken string
That ne'er can sound again, 'tis past and gone,
Its dying sweetness dwells within memory alone —

Year after year with silent lapse fleet by;
Each seems more brief than that which went before;
The weeks of youth are years; but manhood's fly
On swifter wings, years seem but weeks, no more —
So glides a river through a thirsty land,
Wastes as it flows till lost amid the Desert sand.

The green of Spring which melts the heart like love
Is faded long ago, the fiercer light
Of hues autumnal, fire the quivering grove,
And rainbow tints array the mountain-height —
A pomp there is, a glory on the hills
And gold and crimson stream reflected from the rills. [3]

But 'tis a dying pomp a gorgeous shroud
T' enwrap the lifeless year — I scarce forgive
The seeming mockery of death; but that aloud
A voice sounds through my soul — "All things live
To die and die to be renewed again,
Therefore we should rejoice at death and not complain."

Catskill
October, 1837

THE CLOVE, CATSKILLS
1827
Charles F. Smith Fund
The New Britain Museum of American Art
New Britain, Connecticut
Photo: E. Irving Blomstrann

38.

Mother! All hallowed word forever bless'd!
Forever dear to man and most to me,
But utter'd now 'mid sighs but ill suppress'd,
And rising tears that struggle to be free —
Mother! Alas thou dost not answer; 'neath the ground
Thy willing ear is clos'd, nor heedeth mortal sound —

My Mother! Still, the dear, lov'd name I call
It is the natural musick of my tongue,
Sad now its tones, but potent to recall
To mind thy love, thy tenderness, how strong!
And call I vainly? No! The Grave does not enclose
Thy spirit; freed from earth undying it arose —

Hope tells me, and a holy hope like this
Can not be false, whether tis thine to dwell
Beyond the Stars, or in thy blessedness
Dost linger near thy children, lov'd so well,
A Heaven-appointed time; thy kind, maternal care
Still lives — Still thine eye sees us — still thou heard our prayer —

My voice lifts not complaining — Thou art ta'en
From earthly trouble — impious it would be
To wish thee in this darksome world again
To bear with us a sad mortality:
But nature is unconquerable — grief will rise
Within a filial bosom, when a Mother dies.

Not with complaining, but with gratitude
The dear rememberances of love arise —
Thy watchful care with tenderness imbued —
Countless anxieties — self sacrifice —
Wave upon wave till uncontroll'd bursts forth
Thy soul in flattering accents; tribute to thy worth —

                                        October 30, 1837

39.

On the frore [1] shadow of yon mountain-steep
I gaze remembering every tender dye
Of Summer and of Autumn, rich and deep,
The joyous forest's gorgeous pride, and sigh
That the soft seasons speed so swiftly away
And Winter lingers with unkind delay —

I gaze; but not as once 'twas mine to gaze
With heart too full of youthful hope for gloom
Ere those Belov'd Ones we did gently place
Within the confines of the Silent Tomb —
Since then the seasons wear a sadder hue
And Evening's golden tints are faded too —

January 12, 1838

40.

Thine early hopes are fading, one by one,
The brightest, loftiest are the first to die,
Grow faint or cold and perish mournfully.
As in the splendour of the laughing sun
Where mountains put their evening glory on
The burnish'd clouds do gladden all the sky
'Til sunk Day's orb (as my bright youth did merge)
The highest in the Zenith first is dead;
And so successive withering to the verge
Of the drear ocean, until night is spread
And winds and waves chaunt[1] forth their funeral dirge.
Yet thus benighted! Youth's false visions fled!
One changeless Hope remains to cheer my breast,
A lasting Day shall dawn in the resplendant East.[2]

Catskill
March 28, 1838

41.

Thine early Hopes are fading one by one
The brightest loftiest are the first to die
Grow faint; or cold; perish mournfully.
So in the splendor of the joyous sun
The burnished clouds do gladden all the sky
And laughing put their evening-glory on.
Till sunk the orb amid the murmuring surge:
The highest in the concave first is dead
And so successive withering to the verge
Of ocean drear — night's fall is o'er them spread
And winds and waves chaunt forth a funeral dirge.
Yet thus benighted; Youthful visions fled
One changeless hope remains to cheer my breast:
A day will dawn in the Eternal East.

Catskill
[March 28, 1838][1]

42.

And shall I halt midway in my career,[1]
Just as I see the beauteous Fane[2] appear
'Mid th' golden clouds of the horizon far
The Shrine of my devotion and my pilgrimage —
Find neath my feet which yet unwearied are;
Before my eyes undimmed as yet by age
A gulf mysterious whose cloudy depths defy
A passage — Vain are my efforts — Hope is near to die —

July 1, 1838

43.

Thou frail and feeble vine![1]
Year after year I watch with pitying eye
Thy delicate fingers twine
Around that oak, whose sturdy branches high
Wave in the sun, in fruitless vain essay
To rise from the dismal shade to glorious day.

In summer's genial hour
Thy leaves and light-green tendrils stretch aloft
With hope-inspiring power:
But Winter comes too soon and all thy soft
Thy young, gay foilage shrinks in sudden death
And the old stem alone remains beneath.

My fate resembles thine —
I toil to gain a sunnier realm of light
And excellence — waste and pine
In the low shadow of this world of night. —

The genial season sometimes bear me up
'Till hope persuades I ne'er again shall stoop;
But quickly come the withering blast to blight
My rich and prided growth — and I remain
The same low thing to bud — to fade again.

July 22, 1838

44.

I saw a cave of sable[1] depth profound[2]
Oped 'neath a precipice whose awful height
Was lost mid clouds that darkly hung around
Forever hiding from the human sight
Its vast mysterious head — About the mouth
Of the black cavern grisly mosses hung
And clambering herbage in festoons uncouth
Did wildly wave like hair — The stray winds sung
With the rude rock, the tangled growth, the Cavern these
Strains mingled deep — of Lovely Joy of dark Despair —

[October, 1838][3]

45.

Sonnet

O that in adamant[1] were cased my breast!
Or closed mine ear against the distracting noise
Of the great strife political![2] That voice
Which like a hurrying whirlwind comes unblessed
And prostrates man's affections, sympathies,
Domestic joys and duties — makes the Guest
An Enemy and deadly hate has placed
'Twixt Brothers. Holy peace and virtue fly
Before that fierce and multitudinous cry
For Liberty. Dishonored name! Shouts shrill,
Of Selfishness they are and lawless Will.
My soul is sad; for Freedom sinks to die,
Where Party hath usurped her sacred throne
And Love's and Truth's bright Altars overthrown.

November 8, 1838

46.

The Complaint of the Forest [1]

It was a living day, such as makes man
Know that he has a spirit — feel he has a soul
Which is not coop'd up in its mortal clay;
But plays around it like a flame — enjoys
And touches all the visible — communes
And mingles with the elements themselves —
The arch of heaven was darkly deep — no stain
In all that boundless ether sea was seen
And earth sped onward like a sunlit bark
Bound to some distant haven, richly fraught —
The quick fresh air engender'd in those depths
And nurs'd by mountains, held a subtle joy
As though from founts of everlasting health
It gush'd — such vigor giving man's frame
He almost felt himself a god and mov'd along
With an unwonted majesty and power —

    It was in early summer when the earth
    Was wrapp'd in flowers — floating in music made
    By a myriad voices which did sing
    One sweet, one universal song — "Rejoice
    This is the hour when heav'n descends to earth
    Laden with beauty and with love — Rejoice."

I sat beside a lake serene and still
Earth's off'ring to th' imperial sky,
Which the huge heav'nward mountains aloft held
The purest she possest — Around it rose
Walls of indurate rock, that upward swept
Until they quiver'd mid th' Empyrean [2]
An amphitheatre hugely built it seemed
By giants of the primal world, and though
The flood destroyed the mighty builders — hurled
From dizzy heights the ponderous battlements

And crush'd the massive seats; it yet remained
A ruin more sublime than if a thousand
Roman colloseums had been pil'd in one —

And woods deep dark and tangled, rank o'er rank
Upon the pure and peaceful lake look'd down,
A silent people, through the long long years —

'Tis joy which expression has no voice
To sit, when day is sinking, by that lake
To mark the breeze play on the mountain's top
And toss pine and beechen foilage gray;
And from the pink Azalia's fragrant flowers
And violet white 3 haste with its honeyed breath
To kiss with gentle lips the grassy deep;
Bowing the lily to its brim as in the midst
Of the innumerable wavelets it doth seem
A gallant bark with beauty deeply fraught
Careening gaily o'er the dancing waves —

And then to feel that thou art far away
From man's impure resort — from sordid care —
From turmoil and from dust — free as the wind
To muse fond thoughts from worldliness set free.

And twilight o'er that scene so wildly grand
Spread its empurpled wings; with solemn shade
Sublimer far — more deep — more holy too
Than that within dim temples vast and high
Whose clust'ring shafts cast years of anxious care,
And agony and sweat, wrung from the brows
Of groaning multitudes — to gratify
Imperial pomp and pride —

'Twas that bless'd hour
When angels, hov'ring in the crimson clouds,
Commune with man whose grov'lling instincts low
Have been cast off as robes of earthliness
Beside the fount of nature's solitude —

Over my senses stole a deep repose,
And dreams which are but wakefulness of soul,
A brief exemption from encumb'ring earth —
I heard a sound — 'twas wild and strange — a voice
As of ten thousand — musical it was
A gush of richest concord — deep and slow —
A song that fill'd the universal air —

It was the voice of the great Forest that arose
From every valley and dark mountain top
Within the bosom of this mighty land —

Complaint —

Mortal whose love for our umbrageous realms
Exceeds the love of all the race of men;
Whom we have lov'd and for whom have spread
With welcome, our innumerable arms —
Wind fed with fruits of more than earthly taste —
Who from the haunts of men have oftimes fled
To seek consolation in our shades —
Open thine ears! The voice that ne'er before
Was heard by living man — is lifted up
And fills the air — The voice of our complaint —

Thousands —
Thousands of years, yea, they have passed away
As drops of dew upon the sunlit flower;
Or silver vapours on the summer sea —
Thousands of years, like wind-strains on the harp;
Or like forgotten thoughts, have passed away
Unto the bourne 4 of unremembered things —
Thousands of years! when earth first broke
Through Chaos and sprung forth exultingly —
Even then the stars beheld us waving high
Upon the mountains, shining in the vales —
Ere yet the race of man had seen their light.
Before the marble bosom of the earth
Was scarr'd by steel, and granite masses rent

From the precipitous crag, to build a Thebes [5]
Or old Persepolis, [6] whose founders are forgot,
Our arms were clasp'd around the hills, our locks
Shadow'd the streams that lov'd us — our green breasts
Were resting places for the weary clouds —

     All then was harmony and peace — but man
     Arose — he who now vaunts antiquity —
     He the destroyer — amid the shades
     Of oriental realms, destruction's work began —

Echoes [7] whose voice had answered to the call
Of thunder or the winds alone; or to the cry
Of cataracts, sound of sylvan habitants,
Or songs of birds — utter'd responses sharp
And dissonant — the axe — the unresting axe
Incessant smote our venerable ranks,
And crashing branches frequent lash'd the ground.
Stupendous trunks the pride of many years,
Roll'd on the groaning earth with all their umbrage.
Stronger than wintry blasts it swept along
That fierce tornado — stayless perpitual,
Increasing as it flew, until the earth
Our ancient mother lay, blasted and bare
Beneath the burning sun — The little streams
That oft had rais'd their voices in the breeze
In joyful unison with ours, did waste
And pin'd away as though in deep despair —

     Our trackless shades, our dim ubiquity,
     The solemn garb of the primeval world —
     Our glory, our magnificence, was rent —
     And but in difficult places, shelter'd vales
     The remnants of our failing race were found,
     Like scatter'd clouds upon the mountain tops —

The vast Hyrcanian [8] fell and Lebanon's
Dark ranks of Cedar [9] were cut down like grass.
And restless man whose poets sung the joys

Of our green tranquil shades; whose sages taught
That Innocence and Peace, the daughters fair
Of solitude, within our precincts dwelt;
Held not his arm until necessity
Stern master even of him, seiz'd it and bound
And from extinction sav'd our scanty tribes —

Seasons there were when man at war with man
Left us to raze huge cities, desolate
Old Empires and to shed his blood on soil
That once was all our own — When Death had made
All silent, all secure — we would return
And twist our roots around the prostrate shafts
And broken capitals, or strike them deep
Into the soil made richer by man's blood —

Such seasons were but brief, so soon the earth
Again made sanctified by shade, and art
Again resolv'd to nature, man came back,
And once more swept our feeble hosts away —

And yet there was one bright virgin continent
Remote, that Roman name had never reached;
Nor ancient dreams in all their universe —
As inaccessible in primal time
Unto man's thought and eye, as far Uranus [10]
In his secret void — For round it swept
Deep dangerous seas — a homeless waste
Of troubled waves whose everlasting roar
Echo'd in every zone of heaven — whose drear expanse
Spread gloomy, trackless as the midnight sky.

And stories dire of whirlpools fierce and vast
Of stagnant oceans — monsters terrible
That shook the mariner's soul o'er that dread sea
Spread horrour and rais'd a barrier far more strong
Than the unresting tides around that land —
The land of beauty and of many climes —
The land of mighty cataracts — where now
Columbia's eagle flaps her chainless wing —

Thus guarded through long centuries untouch'd
By man — save him our native child whose foot
Disdains the sunbeat soil — who lov'd
Our shafted halls, the covert of the deer —
We flourish'd we rejoic'd — from mountain top
To mountain top we gaz'd and saw o'er vales
And glimm'ring plains our banners green
Wide waving — yet untorn —

                Gladly the spring
On bright and bloomy wing shed fragrance over us, —
And summer laugh'd beneath our verdant roof —
And autumn sigh'd to leave our golden courts.
And when the crimson leaves were strew'd in showers
Upon the broad lap of Oregon wild
Or mighty Huron's wave of Lazuli, [11]
Winter uprais'd his rude and boreal songs,
And we responded in a chorus wild —

O peace primeval! Would that thou hadst staid!
What mov'd thee to unbar thine azure gates
O mighty oceans when the destroyer came? —
Stray'd then thy blasts around Olympus-Air?
Or were they lull'd to breezes round the brain
Of rich Granada's [12] crafty conqueror,
When with pinion strong they should have crushed
Our enemy — And furious smote as when
The fleet of Xerxes [13] on the Grecian coast
Was cast like foam and weed upon the rocks —

But impotent the voice of our complaint:
He came — Few were his numbers first; but soon
The work of desolation was begun,
Close by the heaving main; then on the banks
Of rivers far inland our strength was shorn;
And fire and steel did all their office well —
No stay was there — no rest —

              The tiny cloud
Oft seen in torrid climes, at first sends out
Its puny breezes; but augmenting soon
In darkness and in size — spans the broad sky

With lurid palm and sweeps stupendous o'er
The crashing world — And thus comes rushing on
This human hurricane — which hath no bounds.
E'en this secluded spot our sanctuary,
Which the stern rocks have frowning held aloft
Our enemy has mark'd — These gentle lakes
Shall lose our presence in their limpid flood,
And from the mountains we shall melt away,
Like wreath of mist upon the winds of heaven —
Our doom is near; behold from east to west
The skies are darken'd by ascending smoke,
For every valley is an altar made,
Where unto Mammon [14] and to all the gods
Of man's idolatry, the victims we are.

Missouri's floods are ruffled as by storm,
And Hudson's rugged hills at midnight glow
By light of man-projected meteors —
We feed ten-thousand fires! In one short day
The woodland growth of centuries is consumed,
Our crackling limbs the pond'rous hammer rouse,
With fervent heat — Tormented by our flame
Fierce vapours struggling hiss on every hand —
On Erie's shores — by dusky Arkansaw
Our ranks are falling like the golden grain
In harvest time on Wolga's [15] banks remote —

A few short years these valleys greenly clad,
These slumbering mountains resting in our arms,
Shall naked gleam beneath the scorching sun;
And all their wimpling [16] rivulets be dry —

    No more the deer these bosky [17] dells shall haunt
    Nor squirrel curious chatter near his store —

A few short years! Our ancient race shall be
Like scatter'd Israel's 'mid the tribes of man —

    It ceas'd, that voice, — my answer was in tears.

Catskill
1838

47.

The Lament of the Forest[1]

In joyous Summer, when the exulting earth
Flung fragrance from innumerable flowers
Through the wide wastes of heaven, as on she took
In solitude her everlasting way,
I stood among the mountain heights, alone!
The beauteous mountains, which the voyager
On Hudson's breast far in the purple west
Magnificent beholds; the abutments broad
Whence springs the immeasurable dome of heaven.
A lake was spread before me, so serene
That I had deemed it heaven with silver clouds,
Had not the drowning butterfly, on wing
Of skimming swallow, ever and anon
Wrinkled its glorious face with spreading rings.
It was Earth's offering to the imperial sky
That in their rugged palms the mountains held
Aloft. Around it rose precipitous steeps,
With rock, and crag, and dell, and cavern dank;
Which seemed an amphitheatre hugely built
By mighty Titans when the world was young;
And though the Flood o'erwhelmed the builders, hurled
Downward its loftiest battlements, and crushed
The massive seats, columns and arches vast;
Silent and desolate, it rears on high
A thousand Colosseums heaped in one!
Forests of shadowy pine, hemlock and beech,
And oak and maple ever beautiful,
O'er every rent and boss of ruin spread,
Rank above rank arrayed: the topmost pines
Quivered among the clouds, and on the lake,
Peaceful and calm, the lower woods looked down,
A silent people through the lapsing years.

Beside that lake I lingered long, like one
Who gazes on the face of her he loves,

107

Entranced in thoughts too glad for utterance.
I watched the breeze upon the mountain's breast
Toss the green pine and birchen foliage gray:
The clouds, like angels on their heavenward flight,
Inhaled the perfume from the azalea's flower,
And small white violet, whose honied breath
Made the air sweet, and marked the wavelets break,
Casting the pollen of the rifled flowers
In mimic rage, like gold-dust, on the shores.
The sun descended, and the twilight spread
Its soft empurpled wings; and that blessed hour,
When spirits stooping from the crimson clouds
Commune with man, whose grovelling instincts now
Are laid aside as robes of earthliness
By Nature's pure and solitary fount.

Over my senses stole a sweet repose,
And dreams, which are but wakefulness of soul —
A brief exemption from encumbering clay.
I heard a sound! 'Twas wild and strange; a voice
As of ten thousand! Musical it was —
A gush of richest concord, deep and slow;
A song that filled the universal air!

It was the voice of the great Forest, sent
From every valley and dark mountain top
Within the bosom of this mighty land.

Lament

"Mortal, whose love for our umbrageous realms
Exceeds the love of all the race of man;
Whom we have loved; for who have opened wide
With welcome our innumerable arms;
Open thine ears! The voice that ne'er before
Was heard by living man, is lifted up,
And fills the air — the voice of our complaint.
Thousands of years! — yea, they have passed away
As drops of dew upon the sunlit rose,

Or silver vapors of the summer sea;
Thousands of years! like wind-strains on the harp,
Or like forgotten thoughts, have passed away
Unto the bourne of unremembered things.
Thousands of years! When the fresh earth first broke
Through chaos, swift in new-born joy even then
The stars of heaven beheld us waving high
Upon the mountains, slumbering in the vales:
Or yet the race of man had seen their light,
Before the virgin breast of earth was scarred
By steel, or granite masses rent from rocks
To build vast Thebes or old Persepolis,
Our arms were clasped around the hills, our locks
Shaded the streams that loved us, our green tops
Were resting places for the weary clouds.
Then all was harmony and peace; but Man
Arose — he who now vaunts antiquity —
He the destroyer — and in the sacred shades
Of the far East began destruction's work.
Echo, whose voice had answered to the call
Of thunder or of winds, or to the cry
Of cataracts — sound of sylvan habitants
Or song of birds — uttered responses sharp
And dissonant; the axe unresting smote
Our revered ranks, and crashing branches lashed
The ground, the mighty trunks, the pride of years,
Rolled on the groaning earth with all their umbrage.
Stronger than wintry blasts, and gathering strength,
Swept that tornado, stayless, till the Earth,
Our ancient mother, blasted lay and bare
Beneath the burning sun. The little streams
That oft had raised their voices in the breeze
In joyful unison with ours, did waste
And pine as if in grief that we were not.
Our trackless shades, our dim ubiquity,
In solemn garb of the primeval world,
Our glory, our magnificence, were gone;
And but on difficult places, marsh or steep,
The remnants of our failing race were left,

Like scattered clouds upon the mountain-top.
The vast Hyrcanian wood, and Lebanon's
Dark ranks of cedar were cut down like grass;
And man, whose poets sang our happy shades,
Whose sages taught that Innocence and Peace,
Daughters of Solitude, sojourned in us,
Held not his arm, until Necessity,
Stern master e'en of him, seized it and bound,
And from extinction saved our scanty tribes.

"Seasons there were, when man, at war with man,
Left us to raze proud cities, desolate
Old empires, and pour out his blood on soil
That once was all our own. When death has made
All silent, all secure, we have returned,
Twisted our roots around the prostrate shafts
And broken capitals, or struck them deep
Into the mould made richer by man's blood.
Such seasons were but brief: so soon as earth
Was sanctified again by shade and art,
Again resolved to nature, man came back,
And once more swept our feeble hosts away.

"Yet was there one bright, virgin continent
Remote, that Roman name had never reached,
Nor ancient dreams, in all their universe;
As inaccessible in primal time
To human eye and thought, as Uranus
Far in his secret void. For round it rolled
A troubled deep, whose everlasting roar
Echoed in every zone; whose drear expanse
Spread dark and trackless as the midnight sky;
And stories of vast whirlpools, stagnant seas,
Terrible monsters, that with horror struck
The mariner's soul, these held aloof full long
The roving race of Europe from that land,
The land of beauty and of many climes,
The land of mighty cataracts, where now
Our own proud eagle flaps his chainless wing.

"Thus guarded through long centuries, untouched
By man, save him, our native child, whose foot
Disdained the bleak and sun-beat soil, who loved
Our shafted halls, the covert of the deer,
We flourished, we rejoiced. From mountain top
To mountain top we gazed, and over vales
And glimmering plains we saw our banner green
Wide waving yet untorn. Gladly the Spring
On bloomy wing shed fragrance over us;
And Summer laughed beneath our verdant roof,
And Autumn sighed to leave our golden courts;
And when the crimson leaves were strewn in showers
Upon the ample lap of Oregon,
Or the great Huron's lake of lazuli,
Winter upraised his rude and stormy songs,
And we in a wild chorus answered him.
O prince primeval! would thou hadst remained!
What moved thee to unbar thine emerald gates,
O mighty Deep! when the destroyer came?
Strayed then thy blasts upon Olympus' air,
Or were they lulled to breezes round the brow
Of rich Granada's crafty conqueror,
When with strong wing they should have rushed upon
Our enemy and smitten him, as when
The fleet of Xerxes on the Grecian coast
Was cast like foam and weed upon the rocks!

"But impotent the voice of our complaint:
He came! Few were his numbers first, but soon
The work of desolation was begun
Close by the heaving main; then on the banks
Of rivers inland far, our strength was shorn,
And fire and steel performed their office well.
No stay was there — no rest. The tiny cloud
Oft seen in torrid climes, at first sends forth
A faint light breeze; but gathering as it moves,
Darkness and bulk, it spans the spacious sky
With lurid palm, and sweeps stupendous o'er
The crashing world. And thus comes rushing on

This human hurricane, boundless as swift.
Our sanctuary, this secluded spot,
Which the stern rocks have guarded until now,
Our enemy has marked. This gentle lake
Shall lose our presence in its limpid breast,
And from the mountains we shall melt away,
Like wreaths of mist upon the winds of heaven.
Our doom is near: behold from east to west
The skies are darkened by ascending smoke;
Each hill and every valley is become
An altar unto Mammon, and the gods
Of man's idolatry — the victims we.
Missouri's floods are ruffled as by storm,
And Hudson's rugged hills at midnight glow
By light of man-projected meteors.
We feed ten thousand fires: in our short day
The woodland growth of centuries is consumed;
Our crackling limbs the ponderous hammer rouse
With fervent heat. Tormented by our flame,
Fierce vapors struggling hiss on every hand.
On Erie's shores, by dusky Arkansas,
Our ranks are falling like the heavy grain
In harvest-time on Wolga's distant banks.

"A few short years! — these valleys, greenly clad,
These slumbering mountains, resting in our arms,
Shall naked glare beneath the scorching sun,
And all their wimpling rivulets be dry.
No more the deer shall haunt these bosky glens,
Nor the pert squirrel chatter near his store.
A few short years! — our ancient race shall be,
Like Israel's, scattered 'mong the tribes of men."

112

48.

Oft when o'er Earth is spread the gloomy shade
Of wintry clouds, the ever mournful wind
Sighs like some Ghost that through the forest-glade
Seeketh the quiet it can never find:
So sad, so lost, at times man's spirit flies
From thought to thought yet findeth no relief,
O'ercast by mortal cares that thickening rise,
And Nature all does minister to grief —
O power divine! in such relentless hour
Upon benighted souls thy blessed sunshine pour.

[1838] [1]

49.

Why do ye count your little months, your years,
Or e'en your ages? They are nought: they are
The measure of your feeble breath, your fears.
Ye are as misers, hoarding up with care
A glittering mass, a cold insensate dust,
That ne'er to spirit can be changed: nòr gold,
Nor years are chattles of the soul; they rust,
Or perish: her possession is the trust
In God; the love which tongue hath never told;
And immortality which death shall soon unfold.

December 26, 1839

50.

Upon the bosom of the infant year,[1]
Our First-born! Thou wert brought to earth
The New Year rose — the day-dawn did appear,
And thou dids't breath the breath of life — Thy birth,
The mighty Year's — the Days coeval[2] were —
Auspiciously thy earthly race begun:
No common natal hour was thine, my son! —

Thy name too hath a meaning "Theodore,"
The "Gift of God," that I would ne'er forget;
And may the giver on the gift outpour
His choicest blessings, and before thee set
His shield; so, in the world's tumultuous roar
Thou shalt be strengthened, and sin's arrows fall
Innocuous — thy virtue conquering all —

If 'tis thy lot to live through many years
And this the utterance of a parent's love
Should merit thy gaze — think, think what anxious fears
What hopes, thy Mother's breast and mine did move,
As watching thee with tenderness and tears
We looked into the future, knowing well
That in the world, sorrow and sin do dwell.

And may the love which now I would express
Bring to thine eyes a tear — strength to thy mind
To battle with temptation — onward press
In virtue's path, even for our sakes, and find
In our fond love a cause for lovingness;
And prove my son, when earth's dark vale is trod,
Thou wert indeed the very "Gift of God."

January 1, 1840

51.

The Dial

Gray hairs, unwelcome monitors, begin
To mingle with the locks that shade my brow
And sadly warn me that I stand within
That pale uncertain called the middle age.
Upon the billow's head which soon must bow
I reel; and gaze into the depths where rage
No more the wars 'twixt Time and Life as now,
And gazing swift, descend towards that great Deep
Whose secrets the Almighty one doth keep.

I am as one on mighty errand bound
Uncertain is the distance — fixed the hour;
He stops to gaze upon the Dial's round
Trembling and earnest; when a rising cloud
Casts its oblivious shadow and no more
The gnomon[1] tells us what he would know and loud
Thunders are heard and gathering tempests lower.
Lamenting misspent time he hastes away
And treads again the dim and dubious way.

February 1, 1840

52.

Birdsnest

On topmost bough swinging in every blast
Of Winter's chilliest, keenest breath there hung
A Birdsnest, which nor wind nor hail had cast
From the tough twigs to which it firmly clung.

No twittering such as in the summer's day
I oft have lingering listened to was heard;
But it was empty torn and bleak and gray
The airy cradle of the happy bird.

Far with the summer fled the birdlets gay
Which in that cradle were so fondly tended,
In some unknown and sunnier land they play
Mid bowers where buds and fruits are sweetly blended.

In some far land unknown! Alas!
How like the Hopes my youthful bosom bred;
No mother's care, no love could mine surpass;
But like the birds when winter came they fled,

And left my heart, where they were fondly nursed
Empty and hollow, like yon tossing nest
Sheltering no more nor sheltered from the burst
Of stormy life is now my barren breast.

But I will not repine, Summer will come
Again to bless these groves, again her nest
The bird will build, so let th' unfading bloom
Of Hope surround my idly tortured breast —

Cedar Grove [Catskill]
February, 1840

117

53.

Though snows enwrap the mountain's head
Yet round our feet bright flowers are spread:
O, thus in life may ever be
Sorrow afar — and Joy with thee —

Maria this fond wish of mine
Springs from a love that would entwine
All which is beautiful around
Thy heart in lasting verdure bound.

But sad experience checks the wing
Of Hope — here no eternal Spring
Gladdens the ever changing earth;
Perennial Summer never yet had birth.

I may not hope that life shall be
A lasting sunshine, even to thee:
Clouds, cold and darkness must descend,
And sorrow's self thy anxious spirit bend —

But when life's darkest shadow lays
Upon thy heart, may cheering rays
Of holy hope from out the darkness rise —
A faithful promise of eternal joys —

Thomas Cole
May 10, 1840

54.

Birthday[1]

Thy birthday comes when the meads
Their rich encumbrance to the scythe have given
And tempt to wander when the twilight spreads
Her azure mantle over the earth and heaven.
Amid the glory of the orbed year
The star that rules my heart did first appear.

It was a day of deep import to me
When thou wert born, unconscious though I dwelt
In Youth's unthinking maze. Each hour we see
Weaves in our destiny unseen, unfelt
Some chain of light or shade which shall be found
Forever more about our being bound.

August 3, 1840

55.

The Summer Days are Ended[1]

Summer is gone! The summer days are ended!
A voice mysterious sounded through my ear;
As o'er the hills and through the vales I wended
Rejoicing in the glory of the year.
I paused to listen to the plaint of sadness
It was the wailing of the Autumn wind;
Quick fled my breast its joy and gladness
And sorrow cloud-like brooded o'er my mind.
Wide spread the scene; beauty was still around
And more than beauty; for the glowing earth
In regal crimson and in gold was bound;
And every tree and lowly shrub gave birth
To tents that evening's sun-lit dome no dye
Ethereal shows, their richness could outvie.

I looked into the heavens and they were deep,
Deep as the soul — unfathomed but by God;
A lonely cloud the western gate did keep
As the tired sun night's dusky threshold trod.

The Autumn sky spotless pure is fraught
With melancholy — wild and wandering thought
Pierces the vault; beauty does but veil
The shoreless sea where Doubt and Wonder sail.
There can be gloom in palaces of splendour
Sorrow may dwell the brightest smile beneath
So nature throws a gorgeous robe around her
When chill'd by Winter's sudden grasp of death.

The daylight vanished from the mountain's head
The round moon shone upon the waving woods
And all was silent save the voice that said
With mournful cadence like far-falling floods
"Summer is gone! The Summer days are ended!"
Ere with slow feet my homeward path I wended.

A few short days had passed and forth once more
I ventured for the fresh and healthful air;
I trod the hills and vallies as before;
The vales were cheerless and the hills were bare.

            The wintry blast
     With ruffian hands had torn
     The robe that Earth had worn
            In fragments cast
     It on the miry ground — the floods;
And ruthless shook the loud lamenting woods.
     The floods were riotous and spread
     Their greedy arms o'er grassy plains;
Tore from the husbandman his harvest grains
     And foaming — tossing, swiftly sped
            Down the terrific steep
And plunged in ocean's all-devouring deep.

     Cease! cease proud Floods your laughter
            Your sorrowing shall come after.
            Stern Frost shall forge your chain
            See now upon the winged North he comes!
                 Strong strong as Death! Your struggles vain
            As ghosts unblest among deserted tombs
            With long low smothered groans ye shall complain.

From the deep glen up starts the hoary cliff
Like a grim giant from his gloomy lair
            'Waked by some fiendish scream
            Heard in his horrid dream
Shakes from his brow the dark dishevelled hair
And stares around with icy horror stiff.
For round its granite head the winds are shrieking
The old oaks on its breast are loudly[2] creaking;
Their leaves are shatter'd branches torn
Through air tempestuously borne —
From every dell and rock a voice is breaking —
"Summer is gone! The summer days are ended
And o'er the earth the cold dark months descended."

Yes they are fled Summer and Autumn too!
But shall I grieve and sigh the Winter through?
Bears he no chaplet on his barren [3] brow?
Unfading Ivy, thou dost surely know,
And faithful Evergreens his temples bind;
Pluck them and cast thy sadness to the wind!

   Beside the hearth when winter winds are wild
   Domestic peace and Love and Friendship mild,
   Those Evergreens shall bloom; they flourish best
   When by the storm heart nearer heart is prest.
   Wait God's-own seasons; it would be a curse
   Perennial Summer — Winter is the nurse
   Of Virtue — 'Tis the time to intertwine
   Holy affections and to look within
   The Soul — to strive and win from Time
A wreath that blights nor withers by the change of clime.

                    Thos. Cole
                    1840

56

The Summer Days Are Ended [1]

"Summer is gone! — the summer days are ended!"
　　A voice mysterious struck my wakeful ear,
As o'er the hills and through the vales I wended,
　　Rejoicing in the glory of the year.
I paused to listen to that plaint of sadness;
　　It was the wailing of the Autumn-wind:
Quick fled my breast its airy joy and gladness,
　　And sorrow, cloud-like, brooded o'er my mind.
Wide spread the scene: beauty was still around,
　　And more than beauty; for the glowing earth
In regal crimson and in gold was bound;
　　And evening's colors of ethereal birth,
Were dull, compared with lowly shrub and tree,
Whose hues gushed forth, a fount of harmony.
　　I looked into the heavens, and they were deep,
Deep as the soul; unfathomed, save by God;
　　A lonely cloud the western gate did keep
As the tired sun Night's dusky threshold trod.
The Autumn sky, spotless and pure, is fraught
With melancholy: wild and wandering Thought
Pierces the vault; and Beauty does but veil
The shoreless sea, where Doubt and Wonder sail.
　　There can be gloom in palaces of splendor —
Sorrow may dwell the brightest smile beneath;
　　So Nature throws a gorgeous robe around her,
When chilled by Winter's sudden grasp of death.

The daylight vanished from the mountain's head;
　　The round moon shone upon the waving woods,
And all was silent, save the voice that said,
　　With mournful cadence, like far-falling floods:
"Summer is gone! — the summer days are ended!"
Ere with slow feet my homeward path I wended.

A few short days had passed, and forth once more
    I ventured for the fresh and healthful air:
I trod the hills and valley as before;
      The vales were cheerless, and the hills were bare:
        The wintry blast,
    With ruffian hands, had torn
    The robe that Earth had worn;
        In fragments cast
    It on the miry ground, the floods;
    And ruthless shook the loud-lamenting woods.
      The floods were riotous, and spread
      Their greedy arms o'er grassy plains —
Tore from the husbandman his harvest grains,
And foaming, tossing, swiftly sped
      Down the terrific steep,
    And plunged in Ocean's all-devouring deep.

Cease! cease, proud Floods! your laughter,
Your sorrowing shall come after!
Stern Frost shall forge your chain:
    See now upon the wingèd North he comes,
Strong, strong as Death! Your struggles vain!
    As ghosts unblessed among deserted tombs,
With long, low-smothered groans, shall ye complain!

From the dusk glen up starts the hoary Cliff,
    Like a grim giant from his gloomy lair,
      Waked by some fiendish scream,
      Heard in his horrid dream,
Shakes from his brow the dark dishevelled hair,
    And stares around, with icy horror stiff:
For round its granite head the winds are shrieking,
The old oaks on its breast are harshly creaking;
    Their leaves and clinging branches torn,
    Through air tempestuously borne:
From every dell and rock a voice is breaking:
"Summer is gone! — the summer days are ended,
And o'er the earth the cold dark months descended!"

Yes, they are gone! Summer and Autumn too!
But shall I therefore sigh the winter through?
Bears he no chaplet on his frosty brow?
Unfading Ivy, thou dost surely know,
And faithful Evergreens, his temples bind;
Pluck them, and cast thy sorrows to the wind!

Beside the hearth, when winter winds are wild,
Domestic peace, and love, and friendship mild,
Those *evergreens,* shall bloom; they flourish best
When by the storm heart nearer heart is prest.
Wait God's own seasons; it would be a curse,
Perennial Summer: Winter is the nurse
Of Virtue: 'tis the hour to intertwine
Holy affections, and to look within
The soul; to strive to win from Time
A wreath that withers not by change of clime.

57.

Written upon an Autumnal Leaf

I wish not for the Sybyll's[1] power
To write the dread decrees of fate —
Should not unveil the future hour
The good or ill that on it wait —
But if the mighty skill was mine
To guide the wheels of destiny
Maria, no fond wish of thine
But amply should be granted thee.

[1840][2]

58.

On Another

Beauty doth fade — its emblem is a leaf
That mingles with the earth in quick decay
But virtue like an exaltation bright
Springeth from each to heaven and never dies —

Beauty doth fade — as fades the leaf
Its summer day is bright but brief
But virtue like a star on high
Shines on through all eternity —

[1840] [1]

59.

Like a cloud on the brow of a mountain
When the sun in his glory doth rise;
Like the spray of the far-falling fountain
That ascendeth so swift toward the skies
Like the infant's gay laugh — like the blush
On the virgin's soft cheek — like the flush
Of the floweret that withers anon
Is the year; Yea! the year that is gone. [1]

For the cloud it hath vanished away
Dispersed by the power of the sun
And dissolved in the air is the spray
E're the blue heights of heaven it had won;
And now transient the laugh of the child
And the blush on the virgin's soft cheek
And the flower is of beauty despoiled
E're another bright morning can break.

Like such is the year; it has wings
That bore it with swiftness away
And though round it our memory clings
Ah! we cannot ritard it one day!
It is gone O my soul! It is gone
Its months, weeks and days every one.

Now I turn to the fresh coming year.
Shall wild Hope mount her chariot again?
And rush onward with reckless carreer?
And shall Fancy's bright pictures so vain
Me deceive as may have done before?
Strange delusions! I fear ye and strive
You to cast from my soul evermore;
To escape earth's enchantments and live
In the bondage of truth; for the true

Is the pathway, though weary and sad
And so darksome and dreary to view
That leads up to the world of the glad.

O loved Hope that hath recreant been.
Through the year and the years that are past
Let my chariot wheels turn where is seen
The bright gate of true glory, at last.

                    January 1, 1841

60.

This day hath closed another of my years
And the red current that doth turn the wheel
Of mortal life, of its appointed task
This much hath well performed; to be renewed
No more. I know the years my life has known
I know that there has mingled in their tide
The light, the dark, the painful and the glad;
But when I gaze into the Future's depths
And strive to learn what yet remains of life
Whether of years or hours or seconds, Ah!
'Tis blank, mysterious and mortal ken [1]
Is lost in gloom. Am I disconsolate
That all is dark? Oh God forbid! For though
Not yet is granted prescience to man
Immortal hope is given him to sustain.
Who gave this being knows the time to take.

That time Oh God! I wait! Grant that the hour
Whene'er it come may find me trusting thee.

January 31, 1841

61.

Winds [1]

Winds, that come rushing o'er the distant main,
Whence do you spring, and wither are ye bound?
    I ask in vain!
And why, with ever-mournful sound,
Sweep ye the restless waves, the desert rocks?
    I ask again:
My feeble voice your ceaseless murmur mocks.

Whether upon some icy mountain's head
    Andes or Himmalah, [2]
Roused by the sun, ye first awoke,
    Or on the desert grave
        Of Babylon or Ninevah;
    Or on the Dead Sea's wave
Dreams of the past erst [3] broke
    Your slumber first,
    (Its chain by Terror burst),
I know not: fast ye fled,
And o'er these hills I hear your hurrying tread.

Ye say not whence! Can *any* answer give?
    Mysteriously ye live
Amid the infinite, whose depths untold
The rolling Earth in their vast bosom hold!
Secret your path — unmarked your place of birth.
My soul! art thou not like to these wild winds?
Passing in fitful swiftness o'er the earth —
A wanderer that seeks and never finds!
    My soul replies:
"Look at the ordered skies,
See how each planet keeps its glorious path —
The swift-winged comets do not stray;
The winds have their appointed way,
And so thy spirit hath."

                May, 1841

62.

[Autumn]¹

The yellow forest lies beneath the sun
Quiet, although it suffereth decay
The brooklet to the Ocean-deep does run
With gentle lapse and silent² melts away.
The clouds upon the evening sky are bright
But wasting mingle in the glorious light.

So, may my soul in life's declining hours
Like the still forest never once complain:
And flow unmurmuring adown its course
Like yonder brooklet to the Eternal Main;
And as the clouds upon the sunset sky
Be mingled with the radiance on high.

63.

Autumn

The yellow forest lies beneath the sun
Quiet; although it sufferth decay.
The brooklet to the Ocean-deep does run
With gentle lapse and silent melts away:
The clouds upon the evening sky are bright
But wasting mingle with the glorious light.

So may the soul in life's declining hours
Like the still forest never once complain
And flow unmurmuring adown its course
Like yonder brooklet to the Eternal Main:
And as the clouds upon the sunset sky
Be mingled with the radiance on high.

[1842][1]

64.

Mt. Etna [1]

Breezes and bees were sweetly murmuring
And joyously like children bright,
Bedecked in shining crimson, gold and white,
Frolicked and danced the flowers around my feet.
Those were the fields of Etna where I strayed;
Those were the children of the flowers that erst
Fair Proserpina [2] into garlands wove;
And where yon bubbling waters upward gush
With Pluto sank the loud-lamenting maid.

But these are fables and I lift my eyes
That they may wander through the cloudless sky.
My thoughts' companions; in that deep serene
They soar away 'till in that vast profound
In extacy and wonder they are lost.
What cloud is that, rearing its snowy head,
Dazzling and glorious in the morning sun,
Whose mighty form o'ershadows half the world?
No exaltation of the earth and sea;
It moveth not; nor sun; nor wind disperse;
Nor shatter its indissoluble mass!

Etna! The fastenings of thy lofty tent
Are in the rock-barred earth! Thy roots
Beneath the rushing of the briny deep!
In older times Charybdis [3] furious waved
And Scylla clamored, horrid, at thy feet
But they are wasted by consuming time
Grown old and weak; yet thou, forever young,
Outlivest centuries! Beneath thy gaze
Nations have birth and death. Augmenting ever,
Time that doth crumble temples, pyramids;
Hath watched thee grow until thy regal hand
Usurps the empyrean with its starry realms.
But for yon filmy smoke, that from thy crest

Continual issues; there would be no sign
That from thy mighty breast bursts forth at times
The sulphurous storm — the avalanche of fire;
That midnight is made luminous and day
A ghastly twilight by thy lurid breath.
By thee tormented Earth is tossed and riven;
The shuddering mountains reel; temples and towers
The works of man and man himself, his hopes
His harvests, all, a desolation made!

Sublime art thou O Mount! Whether beneath
The moon in silence sleeping thy woods
And driven snows, and golden fields of corn;
Or bleat upon thy slant breast the gentle flocks,
And shepherds in the mellow flow of eve
Pipe merrily; or when thy scathed sides
Are laved with fire; answered thine earthquake voice
By screams and clamor of affrighted men.
Lone mountain of the pallid brow and heart
Of fire! Thou art a resting place for thought,
Thought reaching far above thy bounds; from thee
To Him who bade the central fires construct
This wond'rous fabric; lifted by thy dread brow
To meet the sun while yet the earth is dark,
And ocean with its ever murmuring waves.

[May, 1842]

65.

Lago Maggiore [1]

O sky and earth! How ye are linked together
Upon the bosom of this gentle lake;
The wild and wandering breeze is doubtful whether
It may your calm and sweet communion break.
'Tis thus within my silent bosom mingle
The memory of distant scenes — my home
And these enchanting prospects; whilst I, single
Companionless, in pensive thought do roam.

The distant and the present sometimes meet
In dream-like hues; but dark thoughts quickly rise
And mar the mirror of the vision sweet
And truth overwhelmeth with a sad surprise:
'Twixt me and those I love an ocean lies
And all the glory of the landscape dies.

June 14, 1842

66.

Life's Pilgrimage [1]

Pilgrim down Life's perilous way
Let thy steps be cautious ever;
For not always is it day,
Sunlight shineth not forever.

Darkness, oftimes, shall surround thee
Unexpected night shall fall
Meteor's dazzling glare confound thee,
Lightening's keen thy soul appal.

Strange the road abrupt and broken,
Ridges, gulfs on every hand
Nought the danger to foretoken
Till upon the brink thou stand.

On the whirlwinds of the mountains
Ghastly phantoms fiercely drive,
In the spray of tortured fountains
Demons hideously live.

Has the floweret's beauty won thee
In the gleam of April-day;
Or the rainbow spread before thee;
Let them tempt thee not to stray.

Should whispering groves, or banks of moss,
Sweet, invite thee to repose;
Sleep would bring thee heavy loss,
Thou art in the midst of foes.

Wary be the Pilgrim ever,
Firm of heart; though weak of limb;
For the body conquers never,
Spirit gains the flight for him.

Though the frame through pain is wasting;
Or in health 'twould lingering stay;
Still the soul is onward hasting:
Time hath never known delay.

Healthful, sickly, buoyant, weary,
Soothed or tossed by joy or ill;
Heartless, mirthful, tearful dreary;
Downward treads the Pilgrim still.

Downward till the pathway endeth
On a shattered precipice;
Far beneath in gloom extendeth
Death's dark shadowy abyss.

Deep the gloom of that dread valley
Thought its depth can never find;
But returneth from the sally
Doleful as the winter-wind.

Off the Pilgrim wildly starteth;
He would fly but turns in vain,
From the craggy shore he parteth,
Plunges ne'er to ride again.

"Is Life's journey then so fearful?
With such perils who shall cope?
Desolate and dark and tearful
Whence shall spring the Pilgrim's hope?

"When unto the gloomy valley
He is worn and weary come
What his fainting spirits rally
If the grave must be his home?"

Pilgrim on Life's perilous way
Keep thy steadfast eye toward Heaven.
'Mid thy perils night and day,
Strength to meet them shall be given.

Peace of heart and holy gladness
From above shall oft descend;
With the deepest of thy sadness
Hope the comforter shall blend.

Angel forms shall hover round thee
And my footsteps gently lead;
Though thick darkness shall surround thee
Safely, surely, shalt thou tread.

So, when reached that valley fearful
On that precipice's brink
Not with shudderings and tearful
Shall thy heart within thee sink.

For with brightening eye uplifted
Gazing o'er the Gulf profound;
Through the clouds dispersed and drifted,
By a light that shines beyond.

Thou shalt see angelic creatures
Clad in sunny splendor stand,
Smiles on their celestial features,
Calling thee to that bright land.

January 1, 1843

67.

A Sunset[1]

I saw a glory in the etherial deep;
A Glory such as from the higher heaven
Must have descended. Earth does never keep
In its embrace such beauty. Clouds were driven
As by the breath of God into strange forms
Unearthly, and did burn with living flames
And hues so bright, so wonderful and rare
That mortal language cannot give them names:
And light and shadow strangely linked their arms
In lovliness; and all continual were
In change; and with each change there came new
    charms.

    Nor orient pearls, nor flowers alive with dew,
    Nor golden tinctures, nor the insect's wing,
    Nor dyes purpureal for imperial view
    Nor all that Art creates, or mortals bring
    Can e'er compare with what the heavens unfurled.
    These are the wings of Angels! I exclaimed,
    Stretched in their mystic beauty o'er the world!
    Let us give thanks to God that in his love
    He grants such glimpses of the world above,
    That we poor pilgrims on this darkling sphere
    Beyond its shadows can our hopes uprear.

                              Catskill
                              October, 1843

68.

On a Sunset Sky[1]

I saw a glory in the sunset deep;
A glory such as from the highest Heaven
Must have descended. Earth does never keep
In its embrace such beauty; Clouds were driven
As by the breath of God into free forms
Unearthly and did burn with living flames
And hues so wonderful, so bright and rare
That mortal language cannot give them names:
And light and shadow strangely linked their arms
In lovliness and all continual were
Changing and with each change there came new charms.
Nor orient pearls; nor flowers fresh with dew
Nor golden tinctures; nor insect's wing
Nor dies purpureal for imperial view;
Nor all that Art or fecund Earth can bring
Can aught compare with what the heavens unfurled.

These are the wings of Angels I exclaimed!
Stretched in their mystic beauty o'er the world!
Let us give thanks to God that in his love
He gives such glimpses of the world above,
That we poor pilgrims on this darkling sphere
Beyond its shadows can our hopes uprear.

October 4, 1843

69.

Winter

Winter hoary, stern and strong
Sits the mountain-crags among
On his bleak and horrid throne
Drift on drift the snow is piled
Which the torturing blasts have thrown
Into forms grotesque and wild —
Ice-ribb'd precipices shed
A cold light o'er his grisly head
Athwart his brows gray clouds are bound
Forever whirling round and round —

  O'er the forests wide he lays his hand
   And they are bare —
  They move and moan a spectral band
   Struck by despair:

He breathes upon the stream, it shrinks from day
And 'neath the ice-heaps seeks its dismal way. [1]

  The lofty pine the Hemlock dark and vast
  Alone defy the cruel Despot's might.
  The ice-rain keen the tempest's withering blast,
  His slaves, assail them fiercely day and night;
  But towering high mid Heaven's vault they stand
  A firm [2] inconquerable band —

When winter closes o'er life's fitful year
And time outspreads a dull and flagging wing
May the Soul's Evergreens thy bosom cheer,
Strong Faith and Hope that ever heavenward spring.

     [1843] [3]

70.

Winter

Winter hoary, stern and strong
Sits the mountain crags among;
On his bleak and horrid throne
Drift on drift the snow is piled
Which the icy blasts have thrown
Into forms grotesque and wild —

Ice-ribb'd precipices shed
Cold light o'er his grisly head;
Clouds athwart his brows are bound
Ever whirling round and round —

O'er forests wide he lays his hand
    And they are bare.
They move and moan a spectral band
    Struck by despair —
He breathes upon the stream it shrinks from day
And seeks 'neath heaped ice its dismal way —
The lofty pine the Hemlock dark and vast
Alone defy the cruel Despot's might —
The ice-rain keen the Tempest's withering blast,
His slaves, assail them day and night;
But towering mid heaven's vault they stand
    A firm unconquerable band —

When winter closes o'er life's fitful year
And Time outspreads a dull and flagging wing
May the soul's Evergreens thy bosom cheer
Strong Faith and Hope that heav'nward spring.

[1843] [1]

VOYAGE OF LIFE: YOUTH
1840
Collection of Munson-Williams-Proctor Institute
Utica, New York

71.

The Voyage of Life[1]

Part One

Forth through the ancient shadowy woods as one
Who hath no being but his thought I wended
Instinctively. The deep and solemn tone,
The holy gloom harmoniously blended
With musings grave and fond of Life and Death
And Immortality; which waits our parting breath.

I dreamed not; but before me rose a wall
Of rock stupendous: crag on crag was piled
In a gray mountainous heap and over all
The towering ramparts shadows fell from wild
Portentous clouds that ever restlessly
Hid the far summits from the wondering eye.

And in the bosom of that stoney pile
Which seemed the ruin of a shattered world
Heaped skyward by some Titan's mighty toil
A cavern yawned like death and changeful curled
Across its sombre arches vast and wide
Pale spectral mists; as though its awful depths to hide.

But yet the eye unwilling to be barred
Pierced far within the antre's[2] silent womb,
Arch beyond arch with many a fissure scarred,
Perceived, until impenetrable gloom
Sealed unto human vision, human thought
The secret things with which its depths were fraught.

From the mysterious bosom of that cave
A gentle river took its winding way,
Reflecting freshly in the crystal wave
Rocks, sky and herbage which the glancing ray
Of the uprising sun made rosy light:
A wreath of glory on the dewy verge[3] of night.

Murmuring it left the dim and shadowy gloom
And joyous as a thing of life it flowed
Where flowers in fragrant companies did bloom
Bespangled all with dew and sweetly bowed
Their beauteous faces o'er the placid stream,
Narcissus-like involved in love's delusive dream.

The song of birds uprose on every side
And mingled sweetly in the jocund air
That frolicked free across the dimpling tide
And o'er that paradise of flowers so fair;
And it did seem as though the sky and earth
Sang choral hymns at some blessed Angel's birth.

Gliding out from the deep recess there came
A wondrous Vessel, golden was its bow,
Which flashed across the waters like a flame.
Of wingèd Hours[4] the Bark was wrought — The prow
A laughing form with such like intertwined;
But dark confused and crowded were the shapes behind.

It bore two beings; one an infant child
That laughed and sported on a flowery bed;
The other was a form of aspect mild;
Radiant it stood and o'er its glorious head
A star hung tremulous and brighter did appear
Than Venus when the morn from cloud and mist is clear.

Its azure wings were poised in buoyant rest
As though just ceased from fanning heavenly air;
One hand the Vessel's rudder graceful pressed,
The other stretched with most benignant care
O'er the child. It was a beauteous form and face
Such like[5] doth meet at Heaven's Gate the soul that findeth grace.

"What meaneth this," with earnest voice I cried,
"The landscape bright, the river's flow serene,
And those two Voyagers —" My soul replied:
"Life hath her pictures of each varied scene
The mortal pilgrim sees, wrought on the heart
In colors clear and strong that never can depart.

146

"Experience is the artist and she toils
Incessantly with ever painful care;
Whether beneath the sun the landscape smiles
Or storms obscure; the lights and shades are there;
But Reason, Passion, Prejudice and Time
Do give the after-tone discordant or sublime.

"By thee now standing midway on the height
Of contemplation not alone are seen
Pictures of the departing past; but sight
Of future scenes is opened through a screen
Of darkling clouds and mists fantastic lies
Across the tearful vision of thy longing eyes.

"By mortal man that River of dark source
Is named the 'Stream of Life'; with constant flow
With many a winding on its downward course,
At times it lags along with motion slow,
At times impetuous o'er the rocky steep
It journeyeth onward toward The Eternal Deep.

"There in that vast Profound — that darkest Dread
That Silence — that immeasurable Gloom,
The Breathless — Shoreless — the Un-islanded
Of the great World — of mighty Time the Tomb
It sinks, it vanishes and mortal eye
Perplexed and troubled, trembling turns on high.

"But human thought, thanks be to God, can soar
Triumphant on the wings of light divine
And take its flight above the Shadow hoar;
Where Angels in a land of beauty shine
In living light which is the Light of Light,
The everlasting day, that suffereth not the night.

"Thou wert such infant Voyager, all men
Have been — the thousands yet unborn will be
Cast in such mould and of such origin
Mysterious to themselves and even he
Who bore our sorrows; for us shed his blood
Was launched in that strange Bark and sailed the mystic flood.

"Know! innocence enshrines the infant-heart
Its tears are but as dew drops freshening joy;
For withering sin, as yet, can claim no part
Nor pale remorse bedim the beaming eye.
Children are buds of Heaven 'tis earthly air
That breeds the cankers, guilt and deadening despair.

"They have their Angels. Yonder dazzling shape
That steers the richly freighted bark is one
Of those who 'minister' and constant keep
A watch around us, leave us not alone
From infancy to age, whether is clear the sky;
Or robed in thunder-clouds dark demons hover high.

"We see them not with our dull mortal eyes,
Yet as Zephyr[6] bears the thistle's down;
Or summer clouds in the cerulean[7] skies,
About us their immaculate arms are thrown,
And nought but Giant Sin can drag us thence
Who grows and conquers by our disobedience."

"O Soul!" I cried! "Why linger not the Hours
In that blest clime of innocence? Why flowed
The stream so swiftly through the land of flowers?
Why did we leave Life's highest hill that glowed
'Mid light celestial? Where the breezes blow
Direct from Heaven, and seek these darker vales below?"

"A higher destiny is thine," replied
My soul "through trial, sorrow, darkness, pain
The road to far sublimer joys does lead
And lasting bliss by suffering we gain
And by the gloomy vale through which we tread
We reach the bliss that makes all earthly joy seem dead."

Part Two

As the broad mountain where the shadows flit
Of clouds dispersing in the summer-breeze;
Or like the eye of one who high does sit
On Taormina's [8] antique height and sees
The fiery Mount [9] afar, the Ruin [10] near at hand,
The flowers, the purple waves that wash the golden strand.

So changed my thought from light to shade;
At times exulting in the glow of hope, at times
In darkness cast by what my soul had said;
'Till sunk in reverie her words seemed chimes
From some far tower, that tell of mystial joy,
Or knell that fills the air as with a lingering sigh.

Again I raised my downcast eyes to look
Upon the scene so beautiful when lo!
The stream no longer from the cavern took
Its gentle way 'tween flowery banks and low
But through a landscape varied, rich and vast
Beneath a sky that dusky cloud had surely never passed.

Wide was the river; with majestic flow
And pomp and power it swept the curving banks
Like some great conqueror whose march is slow
Through tributary lands; while the abasèd ranks,
Shrinking give back on either hand o'erawed
As though they trembling felt the presence of a God.

And like some Wizard's mirror, that displays
The Macrocosm, it did reflect the sky,
Rocks, lawns and mountains with their purple haze,
And living things, the filmy butterfly,
The trembling fawn that drinks, the fluttering dove
And the triumphant eagle soaring far above.

And trees like those which spread their pleasant shade
O'er the green slopes of Eden, and the bowers
Of the once sinless pair, soft, intermingling made
Stood on each shore with branches lifted high
And caught eolian [11] strains that wandered from the sky.

Far, far away the shining river sped
Toward the etherial mountains which did close
Fold beyond fold until they vanished
In the horizon's silver, whence uprose
A structure strangely beautiful and vast
Which every earthly fane [12] Egyptian, Gothic, Greek, surpassed.

It seemed a gorgeous palace in the sky
Such as the glad sun builds above the deep
On summer-eve and lighteth dazzlingly,
Where towering clouds climb up the azure steep
And pinnacles on pinnacles fantastic rise
And ever-changing charm the wondering [13] eyes.

There, rank o'er rank that climbed the crystal air
In horizontal majesty, were crossed
The multitudinous shafts, or ranged afar
Till in the blue perspective they were lost,
And arches linked with arches stretched along
Like to the mystic measures of an antique song.

An antique song whose half-discovered sense
Seems to spring forth from depths, as yet, unknown
And fills the heart with wonder and suspense
Until to thrilling rapture it is grown;
Breathless we listen to each wandering strain
And when the numbers cease, we listen still again.

Above the columned pile sublimely rose
A Dome stupendous; like the moon it shone
When first upon the orient sky she glows
And moves along the Ocean's verge alone;
And yet beyond, above, another sphere
And yet another, vaster, dimly did appear.

As though the blue supernal space were filled
With towers and temples, which the eye intent
Piercing the filmy atmosphere that veiled,
From glorious dome to dome rejoicing went,
And the deep folds of ether were unfurled
To show the splendors of a higher world.

But from the vision of the upper air
My eye descended to the lucid stream;
The wingèd Boat — the Voyagers were there;
But the fair Infant of my earlier dream
Now stood a Youth on manhood's verge, his eye
Flashing with confidence and hot expectancy.

Was lifted toward the sky-encastled scene,
His hand had grasped the helm once gently held
By that Angelic figure so serene,
And eager stretching toward the scene beheld,
His bosom heaved as if with secret powers
Possessed to tread the deep — to outstrip the flying Hours.

With face benignant yet impinged with sorrow,
As oft the sky of eve by melancholy cloud
Which though it doth forbode a stormy morrow
Is not less beautiful, the Angel stood
Upon the bank as from the Boat just freed
And waved her graceful hand and bade the Youth "God Speed."

As one emerging from some misty vale
Meets the glad splendor of the rising sun;
Or mariner who the wintry sea doth sail
Through opening wrack 14 beholds the harbor won,
So did I gaze upon the charming scene
And in my joy forgot the vision Infantine.

When thus the Voice in plantive accents mild:
"Ah simple mortal Earth has many a show
That passes quickly — thou a credulous child,
All men are children and they thoughtless go
Through life's strange vale lingering by every flower
Forgetful life is labor and its term an hour.

"The scene before thee beautiful and bright
Is but a phantasm of Youth's heated brain
And doomed to fade as day before the night;
Fleeting its glory, transitory, vain;
Save that it teaches the meek humble soul
Earth's grandeur ne'er should be the spirit's Goal.

"Not that the earth foundationless is laid,
An unsubstantial thing, a cloud, a mist;
But 'tis a darkling soil wherein the seed
Of Virtue planted, tended may subsist
And washed by many tears may grow
To more enduring beauty than these gauds below.

"But mark the Youth, how filled his eager eye
With the bright exaltation. — See! he aims
To reach the portal of the palace high
Above whose cloudy arch resplendant flames
The tempting semblance of a conqueror's crown
And wreath to bind the brows of him who wins renown.

"And while he gazes greater glories rise
Higher yet higher; ardent young desire
With telescopic vision fills the skies.
Gay are the banks in verdurous attire
And swift the river floweth toward his hope
The palace stands beyond, reached by a gentle slope.

"Weak and deluded one! Dost thou not know
Thy Bark is hasting down the Stream of Life
And tarries not for any golden show
In pleasure's gardens though with beauty rife!
So doth the comet pass the planets by
Nor rests; but speeds on its appointed destiny.

"Does not thine eye perceive that when yon towers
Are well nigh gained with sudden sweep the stream,
And growing swiftness, shoots away and pours
Impetuous, towards a shadowy ravine deep
Cleft in the mountain's vast and misty side
As though it eager sought its thwarted floods to hide."

The voice had paused: "And is it thus" I cried,
"That Youth's fond hopes must ever pass away;
As empty dreams, untouched unsatisfied:
Why leaves the Angel on his dangerous way
The Voyager? That hand divine could steer
The willing Boat to where yon glittering domes uprear.

"And lingering by these fresh and verdant shores
E'en youth might live a long long life of joy
And shun perchance the torrent where it pours
Adown yon dread descent." To which reply
Came quickly, "Shrouded as now thou art in earth
Thou canst not see the end for which came mortal birth.

"In the Almighty mind the secret cause is laid;
This must thou learn, that our brief mortal life
Nor rests nor lingers; nor is checked nor stayed
By human skill or might howe'er so rife;
Nor is it in an Angel's godlike power
To lengthen out its wasting thread one single hour.

"Through feeble Infancy is steered the Bark of Life
By Angel hands; but growing man demands
The helm in confidence and dares the strife
Of the far-sweeping waves. The lurking sands,
The rapids foaming through the channel dim,
The roaring cataract are all unknown to him.

"Wisdom is born of sorrow and of care
And from man's conflicts with the world arise
A sense of weakness and of chilling fear
And driven from earth his hopes ascend the skies.
Thus is he launched upon the stream alone
To chasten pride and give young desire a holier tone.

"He is alone; but still deserted never
The Angel yet shall watch his perilous way;
And though the clouds of earth may seem to sever,
Still through the darkness shines the Angelic ray;
And in the hour of midnight o'er the deep
The Guardian Spirit kind will constant vigil keep."

Part Three

Those closing accents fell upon my ear
Sweetly as dew upon the drooping flower
For in my thoughts were knit suspense and fear
Which grew to hope transmuted by their power,
So the first breeze of Spring upon the hills
With sighs awakes the buds and frees the ice-bound rills.

In gentle reverie my mind reposed
When lo! The vision changed — A dismal vale —
Its sides down stooping into night were bossed
With jagged rocks — above huge crags rose pale
And quivering in thick turbulent air
Like hell-affrighted spectres starting from their lair.

It seemed the Earthquake there had oped his jaws
And fierce Convulsion rent the ribs of Earth;
Darkness and light forgot their ancient laws.
It was a den where demons had their birth
Where voices strange and many a dusky form
Smote the strained ear and did the sky [15] deform.

And down this valley's gulphy depths profound;
Where resting place is none; nor green retreat;
Where fear and death forever hover round,
On every blast their restless pinions beat;
The river of my Vision took its way
And left far-far behind the golden light of day.

Onward it dashed and with a tyrannic [16] force
Swept o'er the fractured rocks and foamed and fell
And reeled from side to side with thunders hoarse:
Though broken off and baffled naught could quell: —
Athwart the steep the streaming floods did pour
And rocky fragments fell, dislodged amid the roar.

On a swift curve, a verge of glossy green,
Such Niagaras where its waters leap
The dizzy precipice, the Boat was seen
Fleet as a meteor thwart the midnight deep.
Like famished wolves when the scared prey is nigh,
The pale demoniac floods roared louder as for joy.

No more youth's sunshine like a halo spread
Around the Voyager's high imperial brow;
But Care's wan shadow settled on his head
As clouds their gloom upon the mountain throw.
His now the middle age when human thought
Ascends her highest tower with rich experience fraught.

So have we seen in some dense city's way
A frantic steed dash through the affrighted crowd
With his pale rider — to and fro they sway
With headlong speed mid shrieks and clamor loud
'Till by a sudden plunge he disappears. —
In dumb suspense we stand and quake with horrid fears.

"What now can save?" I cried. O ever blind
But to the present and the mask of things
Was quick replied: "Doubter! Thou yet mayest find
That what appears the greatest evil brings
Supremest good as blackest storms and rain
Bring freshness, beauty, glory in their passing train.

"Behold the Guardian Angel sitteth yet
Benignant 'mong the stormy clouds aloft
Kindling their blackness; like a Glory set
By God in midnight space — A sun whose soft
Unbroken light illumes some lonely sphere
That travelleth through depths of trackless ether drear.

"She waits with joy the prayer which heavenward now
The Voyager uplifts — Faith's earnest cry:
For rescued by that act the floods below
With all their fury; nor the tempest nigh;
Nor ocean, seen afar have power to harm;
Nor yet yon Demon Shapes terrific cause alarm.

"This is the crisis — this the decisive hour
In life's swift fever — balance Life and Death.
Adversity's cold storm and Sorrow's power
Temptation desperate with changeful breath
Break with unmitigated fury on the Man,
And Pleasure once so fair is sicklied o'er and wan.

155

"And earthly hopes are wrecked and cherished joy;
And friends estranged; or turned to foes; or gone
Youth's crown of Glory faded and for aye:
O'er Earth o'er Heaven a dusky pall is thrown:
Affection's treasured things are found to fly
Sink in the silent tomb, or vanish witheringly.

"Young Love's delicious river soon ran dry
And wasted in life's wilderness of drought;
Ambition that once filled the ample sky
Was but a dazzling cloud with tempest fraught:
All, perished in the World or lost in Death
As wastes in frosty air the warm and vaporous breath.

"The heart doth suffer violence, racked and riven
By the relentless blasts of earthly ill.
Burthened with sin all vainly hath it striven
Like a huge oak upon a wind-swept hill
As tortured branches lash the Autumnal gale
And struggling yield their umbrage with a lengthened wail.

"But as the Spring, the gentle Spring, draws nigh
To warm its mighty heart and swell its buds
To lift its fragrance and to beautify;
So through the Voyager's breast, amid these floods,
A living warmth shall steal and prayer shall rise
And yon attendant Spirit waft it to the skies.

"The Guardian watches yet the weltering bark
O'er the vexed floods adown the dizzy steep
Through rock-ribbed channels hideous and dark
Safely to guide him toward yon Ocean deep
Whose darkly boundless waves eternal silence keep."

My Teacher! Guide! Thou who hast kindly read
The meaning of these wondrous scenes to me
Still my heart trembles, like a fragile reed
By the lone shore where stamps the angry sea,
This is a fearful-over-perilous way
To lead but to yon Ocean's misty horror gray.

156

And must the Voyager, these perils past
Dwell ever on that vast and gloomy main,
And on its lethean [17] bosom dull be cast,
Dreamless, eternally to sleep? Then vain
Would seem his Birth, his Youth, his Manhood prime;
Strange, useless burthens on the drooping Wings of Time.

"Yet! Yet distrustful and forgetful ever
Dull to the voice of wisdom! I have said,
Death's pallid hand the cloudy veil shall sever
And wonder Ocean widely, darkly spread,
Be as a curtain quickly drawn away
And open like the Morn for a surpassing day."

Part Four

Struck by my Mentor's serious reply
In sorrow I had clasped my hoods across
My tearful eyes; yet were my tears half joy;
For the quick sentence of rebuke did close
With breath of kindling hope and promise bright;
As broke upon the blind by Siloam's [18] pool of light.

"Behold!" the voice then said: "The closing scene
Of best humanity." The winds had ceased
Their raving and the floods their roar — serene
The air yet steeped in gloom as is the East
When Earth's broad shadow o'er itself extends
And far beneath the Main the evening sun descends.

No hills of green, no gentle flowery vales
No breezes fresh from out the crystal deeps
No blithe birds warbling oft repeated tales;
But silence, leaden silence, such as keeps
The tongue fast bound the straining ear awakes
As when the judge's sentence on the prisoner breaks.

There, flowed the river; but with sluggish pace
And met and mingled with the Ocean dun [19]
No more exulting in the headlong race;
But fainting as its destined Goal was won —
Last 'mid the boundless, as the single voice
When crowded multitudes do suffer; or rejoice.

Still the eye caught the dim and shadowy shore,
The last bare headlands of the dark terrene;
Herbless, desolate, glimmering and obscure;
As landscape by the troubled dreamer seen,
Their shattered forms down sinking one by one
Into the deep of many deeps, the fathomless unknown.

Oppressed I gazed: my thick and struggling sighs
Or checked by the silence would have filled the air;
But soon the winged Boat my eager eyes
Discerned — the Man — the Tempest-tossed was there.
O'er the unrippled flood with motion slow
As heavy laden, sinking — sinking moved the prow.

Broken that prow which once glanced o'er the stream;
Its Hours ensculptured all in gold were gone,
And gushed the floods through many a gaping seam:
It stopped, — it settled — like a thing of stone: —
Some ponderous rock that 'cross the plain is sent;
Which labors on and on 'till with its labor spent.

There sat the Voyager, an ancient Man,
Withered and blighted by the frosts of time:
Furrowed his cheek, his forehead bare and wan
As though the tempests of each earthly clime
Had broken o'er him in their fiercest mood
And he with patient soul their fury had withstood.

Then as the fulgent [20] moon o'er ocean comes,
Spreading her wings of light at eventide,
I saw the Guardian's radiant flames
Hush the black midnight wave and swiftly glide
Through the illumined, fast dissolving wrack
And by the Voyager her airy station take.

The Old man saw the Spirit for the earth
Was falling from his soul and from his eyes
The film of blinding clay as falls the swarth
Envelope from the opening bud. Surprise!
O blest! To see, undreaming, spirit forms
Immaculate and free from all that earth deforms.

He saw the blessed Guardian of his way
And knew "his Angel"; ne'er before discerned;
And love and new-born joy broke in like day
Upon his heaven-illumined soul. He turned
To gaze upon the beauteous one, when lo!
As from the clouds strange music 'gan to flow.

Music it was, if thus is named in heaven
Those mingled gushes of Seraphic [21] bliss
Which flowed like sunlight of the Spring-tide given
In beamy gold to wake the wilderness;
Or like the hymning of some circling band
Of joyous stars just sped from their Creator's hand.

Gently swelling, gently falling
Softer, sweeter yet it grows;
As when Summer's breeze is calling
Fragrance from the dewy rose.
Yes far sweeter and more thrilling
Were the soulèd sounds that fell,
All the airy concave filling
And the heart's most secret cell.
Tuneful breathings — voicèd hymning
Joined with harps of golden sound
Fill the spherèd concave brimming —
Shed rich harmony around.
Now the Trumpet's crystal voice
Lifteth up its notes of joy
Calling to the saved "Rejoice!
Enter through Heaven's portal high."
Back the murky clouds are driven
As the blackness of the sky
By the morning sun is riven

Angels! Angels! Blessed creatures!
Toward the Voyager descend;
Turn on him their holy features
Lit by joy that ne'er can end;
Down the streamy light they sweep
Round him wave their dazzling wings; —
Lift him gently from the deep
Whisper to him wondrous things.
Swift he rises — Earth has left him
With its painful load of clay; —
Death or grief and sin hath reft[22] him
And he soars — away! — away!

I turned mine eyes; I could no longer gaze
Upon the Splendour, which intenser grew
And live; To my relief a dimming haze
Dropt like a curtain dark and shut the view;
But 'neath the weight of Glory which had shone
Upon the Earth's low bosom prostrate I was thrown.

There long I lay mingling my sighs and tears
Recalling all the Vision to my mind,
Its varied scenes, its many hopes and fears
Its seasons four mysteriously combined,
How through bright Childhood's vale the river flowed
Youth, Manhood, Age, to reach[23] the mighty flood.

But my soul spoke and roused me — "Rise
Dwell not inactive on the Vision true
Remember that Life's River swiftly hies[24]
Toward the great Deep and thou hast much to do:
The Vision teaches when divined aright
That he must trust in God and strike,
        who conquers in the fight."

Catskill
June 14, 1844

160

72.

These shady groves, these bright blue hills
From memory ne'er can pass away
Though borne afar by winds and waves
I visit realms of earlier day

Within my heart I e'er shall feel
The breezes of these vallies blow
Each rippling lake, each glancing rill
Will murmur wheresoe'er I go.

No! These wild mountain streams and woods
Have grown so beauteous to my soul
That life's swift stream reflects them clear
Where'er its wandering waters roll.

Catskill Mountains
1845

73.

The March of Time

Hark! I heard the tread of Time
O'er heaven's ether fields sublime;
Through the portals of the Past;
Where the stars by God were cast
O'er the illimitable vast!

Onward! Onward! Yet he strides;
Nations clinging to his sides
Kingdoms crushed, he tramples o'er:
Fame's shrill trumpet — War's deep roar
Blast-like rise — then speak no more.

Lo he nears us! Like a cloud,
Which the trembling sea doth shroud,
Darkly folding every flower
Of our life; Hope, Love and Power
Ah! he grasps the present hour!

Grasps it — it is withering
Hangs a misty faded thing
In his girdle seen no more
But by deeds that stud it o'er
These shall mark it evermore.

On he passes swift as fear
Hiding each faint struggling year
Neath his pinion's shadowy fold
All that sky and earth do hold.
Much which man may not behold.

Lo! beneath his mantle dark
Grim, a spectre pallid, stark
Clingeth round him like a sheath

Powerful; yet devoid of breath —
Throwing darts! 'Tis death! 'Tis death.

Stop the ruffian Time! Lay hold!
Hath Heaven nor Earth power so bold!
As to meet his strength midway,
Wrest from him the precious prey
And the Tyrant-Robber slay.

Struggle not my foolish soul
Let Time's garments round thee roll.
Time God's servant think no scorn,
Gathers up the sheaths of corn
Which the spectre Death hath shorn.

And anon shall One appear
Brighter than the Morning Star
Who shall smite that Spectre frore.[1]
Time shall, clasped by death no more,
Take a new name — Evermore.

1843

74.

The March of Time

Hark! I heard the tread of Time
Marching o'er the fields sublime;
Through the portals of the past
When the stars by God were cast
O'er the illimitable vast.

Onward! Onward yet he strides
Nations clinging to his sides.
Kingdoms crushed he tramples o'er
Fame's shrill Trumpet — War's deep Roar
Blast-like rise — sound[1] no more.

Lo! he nears as like a cloud;
That the trembling sea doth shroud,
Darkly folding every flower
Of our Life; — Love — Hope and Power:
See! He grasps the Present Hour!

Grasps it — it is withering
And it hangs a faded thing
In his girdle; seen no more
But by deeds that stud it o'er —
These shall mark it evermore.

On he passes, swift as fear;
Hides each faint and fleeting year
In his pinion's shadowy fold; —
All that sky and earth do hold: —
Things which man may not behold.

Lo! beneath his mantle dark
Grim, a spectre pallid stark
Clings around him like a sheath

Mighty! though devoid of breath
Throwing darts: — 'Tis Death! 'Tis Death.

Stop the Ruffian Time! Lay hold!
Is there then no power so bold!
None to meet his strength midway —
Wrest from him his precious prey,
And the Tyrant-Robber slay.

Struggle not my foolish soul!
Let Time's garments round thee roll:
Time, God's servant, think no scorn,
Gathers up the sheaves of corn
Which the spectre Death hath shorn.

And anon shall one appear
Brighter than the Morning Star:
He shall smite that Spectre frore
Time shall, clasped by Death no more,
Take a new name — Evermore.

Catskill
February 3, 1846

75.

Just before Sunrise

Rise from thy slumbers thou of counted years;
Nor let the precious light fall on thy couch
Like dews of heaven on a withered tree
With profitless and unrefreshful waste.
Rise! For the sun hath breathed upon the sky
And the cold ether through its orient depths
Melts like dusk metal in the forge's flame
Rise! For the sun has full nigh climbed the wall
Of horizontal amethyst and swift
Unbars the gates of day. Rise ere he rises!
'Tis the choice moment of unnumbered hours.
Cloudless the ether — deeper and more deep
It grows — The piercing eye amazed is lost
And life itself will not suffice to sound
Depths that are infinite. See the wan moon
Above the western steeps like a faint maiden
Sinks 'mid her purple curtains to repose.
And yonder mountains speechless as with awe
Upturn their holy faces to the sky.

Be still! For in this sacred solemn deep
Of silence all things mute do pray.
                              Amen!!

                    October 27, 1847

76.

The Cross

O Sacred symbol of our Faith!
Despised in this dark day
By those who leave the narrow path
To seek an easier way.

To there raise my streaming eyes
From Life's Tempestuous vale
Where Sin's deep midnight-shadow lies
And driving griefs assail.

Thou art the dawn to my blessed sight
That o'er the mountains breaks
Already by thy holy light
My soul triumphant wakes.

We know thy growing light a sign
The sun himself is nigh;
The sun of Righteousness divine
Ascends the glorious sky.

At Eve he sank beneath the shade;
But on dark Calvary's height
Thy form a moon refulgent made
By his transforming light —

Brighter and brighter grows the cross
The mountain-tops are gold
And o'er death's vally far across
The gorgeous light is rolled.

1848

77.

Alone Yet Not Alone[1]

The desert flower afar may bloom
Where foot of man ne'er trod
Yet gracefully its soft perfume
Ascendeth up to God
   And He will own the offering too,
   And fills its cup with living dew.

Alone may sing the forest bird
   Afar from human ear,
Yet there he singeth not unheard,
   For God is listening near;
And He will cheer the warbler's breast,
With pleasant food and quiet rest.

Thus when before His gracious throne,
   With grateful praise I bend;
I feel I am not all alone,
   For God is still my friend;
And humble though my love may be,
He answereth it with love to me.

Each morn will bring a promise pure,
   As dew to desert flower;
Each eve a rest as calm and pure,
   As birds in forest bower;
Till death shall free my earth-bound wing,
And bear me heavenward as I sing.

78.

A Painter

I know 'tis vain ye mountains, and ye woods
To strive to match your wild, and wonderous hues,
Ye rocks and lakes, and ever rolling floods,
The gold-cinctur'd eve, or morn begemm'd with dews —

Yes, day by day and year by year I've toil'd
In the lone chamber,[1] and the sunny field
To grasp[2] your beauty; but I have been foil'd —
I cannot conquer; but I will not yield —

How oft have I, where spread the pictur'd scene
Wrought on the canvas with fond, anxious care,
Deemed I had equalled nature's forests green,
Her lakes, her rocks, and e'en the ambient air.

Vain unpious thought! such feverish fancies sweep
Swift from the brain — when nature's landscapes break
Upon the thrilling sense — O I could weep
Not that she is so beautiful; but I so weak —

O! for a power to snatch the living light
From heaven, and darkness from some deep abyss,
Made palpable: with skill to mingle right
Their mystery of beauty! then mine would be bliss!

79.

Evening

See the sun all gold and red
Leaves the blue and open sky
Sinking to his glorious bed
Far beyond the mountains high.

He has travelled all the day
Over land and over sea
Cheering with his pleasant ray
All the living things that be.

He the paths of men has lighted
And the forests and the flowers
Which without his beams were blighted
By the long long darksome hours.

Now the lofty mountain hides
Half the bright face of the sun
Downward and downward yet he glides —
Now his daily journey's done.

But to-morrow in the sky
When the dewy morn shall come
We shall see his shining eye
Light again our pleasant home.

Little children should take warning
By the ever faithful sun
Praise God who made the Sun, Night and Morning
As their daily course is run.

80.

Life

Life is the keeper of the gate called Death,
Leadeth us there and ope's the gloomy door
Taketh thereat the toll, our mortal breath;
Then journeys on with us forever more.

Life is the mortal house where dwells the soul
Upon the margin of eternal time
One side is bared when waves of trouble roll;
The other stands 'mid silent deeps sublime.

Life is the air we breathe, the things around
We see and feel — these are its mortal load
Death touches us, they pass and with a bound
We spring aloft to seek a new abode.

Life is our all — this little vale of tears[1]
Is but the vestibule where we unrobe,
Death lifts the curtain and beyond appears
The Life of Life that is not of our globe.

Life! Life! Which way we look is Life. Death
Is but the shadow of our sin on Life;
That dims the glass of being like a breath;
But Heaven shall shine upon the shade and Life
Be free from strain, and brighter be through Death.

81.

Lines occasioned by the death of Miss M. A. W.

The greedy tomb hath op'ned once again
To snatch away that which we dearly prize
Our loves our friendships, all, alas! seem vain
For all we love, and cherish, quickly dies —

Death the unsparing hath again stretch'd forth
His icy hand — blighted a budding flower.
So young, so beautiful, of so much worth
We almost deem'd her rais'd beyond his power.

The undrain'd cup of life from which she drank
Was at its sweetest when 'twas dash'd away
The flower was just at opening as it sank
Beneath the chilling blight's untimely sway.

"Mourn not the virtuous dead": it hath been spoken;
But what shall stop the sluices of our grief;
Or heal affection's wounds so newly broken;
Or offer to our hearts a quick relief —

Not for her sake break forth our sighs of wo
(She dwells in bliss supreme) but for our own,
Still bound by earthly chains, to pains below,
Wilst she exalted sits beside th' Almighty's throne.

T. Cole

172

82.

Lines suggested by a picture painted by Weir,[1]
in which a lady is seen sitting at a window
gazing on the sea, whilst a youth at her side
is playing the guitar —

A lady sat by a window high
    And gaz'd upon the sea
The tear drops came in her beauteous eye
    And hung there tremblingly.

And a gallant youth was at her side:
    He looked not on the sea
But touching the sweet guitar he cried
    "Oh lady! list to me."

"For thy beauty is to me the world
    My love a drainless sea,
Pure as the sky that is now unfurl'd
    A stainless canopy.

"Oh turn those eyes, which are my heav'n
    From off the vacant sea
Let not thy tears to the waves be given
    On my bosom let them be."

She heard not though truth with music fell
    But still gaz'd on the sea
For where the mind delights to dwell
    The eyes would gladly be.

Her heart is with yon lessening sail
    As it fades o'er the sea,
And if a loving maiden's tears avail
    'Twill glide on pleasantly?

And swift for the sake of one it hears
    Return o'er the quiet sea,
And grief the source of those flowing tears
    Be chang'd to extacy.

83.

Lines Suggested by a Voyage up the
Hudson on a Moonlight Night —

Midnight the hour when silence sleeps
When o'er dim vales and craggy steeps
The viewless spirits of the sky
Pour from their starry urns on high
The pearly dew; each bud and flower
Moistens its bosom in the shower
And every fay [1] his goblet fills
With nectar which the heaven distils —

Hudson! The breeze has ceased to press
Thy wave! And on its placidness
The moonbeams are caress'd, and lie
Bright sleeping undisturbedly
Ever should loveliness recline
On couch as beautiful as thine —

From out thy depths the mountains rise
And lift their shadows to the skies —
In silent awfulness they tower
Like spectres that by magic power
Are call'd from some vast black abyss
Cav'd in earth's bosom bottomless,
Whilst round each huge brow rough and sear
The moonlight trembles as in fear.

Yon moonlit bark beneath the hill
Hath not a breeze its sail to fill
But gently on the ebbing flood
It glides past mountain rock and wood
'Tis like yon cloud that moves on high
Alone — no other cloud is nigh.
The winds are still but on it springs

Borne by its own aerial wings —
I love this stilly hour of night
For fancy's visions are more bright
Than in the troubled glare of day
With all its pomp and proud display —
Midnight hath loosed the chain that bound
The spirit to its earthly round —

TC

84.

Lines suggested by hearing Music
on the Boston Common at night

Music it was I heard, and music too
Of mortal utterance; but it did sound
Unto my Fancy's ear like that of spirits;
Spirits that dwell within the vasty caves
Near the earth's center —
                              Silence dwelt around.
Then came soft sounds slowly, with pauses 'twixt
Like sighs of sleepers in deep distant caves
They sank and list'ning silence reign'd again.

Then rose a voice, a single voice but shrill
It rent the sable curtains of the gloom
And pierc'd the confines of each echoing cave,
And ev'ry spirit rais'd his sleepy head
From the cold pillow of the dripping rock —
Again the single voice, rang with a shriller tone,
Each spirit answer'd from his hidden nook —
Some voices came from distant winding cliffs
And sought the ear like angel whisperings.
From the deep arches of the rocky roof
Tones rich as those of heav'n's own trumpets burst.
From out the dark profound abyss arose
Sounds as of earthquake, thunder, or the roar
Of booming cataracts — silence again —

Hark! They have met within the giant hall:
Whose roof is pillar'd by huge mountain tops,
And voices shrill, and deep in concord loudly join.
The heaving harmony sweeps to and fro
Surge over surge and fills the ample place.
Ocean of sound sublime!! The tides contend,
Augment, higher, yet higher; Earth cannot
Contain; it yields — 'tis riven — and falling rocks

And tottering pinnacles join their dread voices
In the tumultuous and astounding roar —

'Tis past. And nought now strikes the waiting ear
Save the soft echoes ling'ring on their way.
Soft! They have ceas'd to whisper, having found
The cave of silence their eternal tomb.

T. C.

85.

Morning

See how shines the morning light
Gently on each tree and flower!
God hath kept them safe all night
By his goodness and his power.

Through the long, dark hours gone by
While we all were fast asleep
God with his all-seeing eye
From all danger did us keep.

On the trees that stand close by
Birds their little voices raise
Singing to the Lord on high
In sweet strains of thankful praise.

Like the birds with cheerful voice,
When the morning lights the sky,
Our own simple songs should rise
      Unto God who dwells on high.

VIEW OF THE FALLS OF MUNDA
NEAR PORTAGE ON THE GENESEE FALLS, N. Y.
1847
Jesse Metcalf Fund
The Museum of Art, Rhode Island School of Design
Providence, Rhode Island

86.

The Burial Ground at Catskill

The hill is climb'd and this the place of rest —
Here, among tombs beneath whose simple shade
Sleep those who wake not, when the eastern light
Streams o'er the hills, and gilds the silky grass
That waves, and whispers o'er their lowly bed.
Close are the earthy curtains that surround
Them drawn and not a single ray can pierce
The silent valley of their deep repose —
They need it not, — their tasks of toil are o'er —
No more the voice of friendship or of love
Calls them to gaze upon the glorious morn —
But oft a mourner o'er the simple tomb
Woos from his memory lov'd and cherish'd things
And as each image rises from the deep
The fount of sorrow gushes forth afresh —
This is indeed a place of rest and such
Would be my choice if heav'n would grant my boon,
To be sepulchred here — to rest upon
The spot of earth that living I have lov'd.
No marble pile, no vaunting verse I wish
To mark my resting place to tell the world
Of virtues that I ne'er possess'd — for pomp
An icier chill gives to the cold clay —
But here! beneath the solemn dome of heaven,
Where the free winds forever warble wild
Where yon far mountains steep; would constant look
Upon the grave of one who lov'd to gaze on them —

O! I have stood here when the westering sun
Had placed a glory on the scene and gaz'd
Upon the mountains woods, and sky, until
My spirit disenthralled, forgot its clay —
It moved among the mountains and amid
The clouds rejoicing held its way.

87.

The Lute

One day I fled the tainted crowd
And wandered far away
To where the wild woods' sombre shroud
Shut out the light of day.

And when the solitude was mine
On gray, fantastic root
I sat; of old and hoary pine
And struck my mournful lute.

An antique Lute it was I brought
From a far, tuneful land
With a wild melody 'twas fraught
When struck with skilful hand.

For it had Music's spirit bound
Within its stringèd zone
Which seemed when sank its native ground
To take a sorrowing tone.

How much of Heaven there can be
Wrapped in the fashioned wood!
The wind-songs of the parent tree
Thrilled yet in mournful mood.

The weary world was far away
The world of care and pain
And pride was far and pomp's display,
That vex the tortured brain.

My swelling voice with power did rise
And stirred the sleepy air;
The timorous deer with star-like eyes
Stood still and listened there.

I sang my heart; for it was full
The world had wronged it so
And sad and unrequited love
Had wrought it much of woe.

I called the rocks and streamlets near
To listen to my strain
And bade the woodland spirits hear!
I did not sing in vain.

I sang "I cast the world behind
To worship in your Fane
Ambition ne'er shall rule my mind
Nor Love imperious reign.

"The face of man no more I'll see;
But live and die in peace
And learn to love the flower and tree
And tend their lovliness.

"The deer shall my companion be
Attendant at my side —
The squirrel leave the lofty tree
And in my cot abide.

"That cot of branches shall be made
With roof of matted pine
And on its floor soft masses laid
Inviting to recline.

"The streamlet gurgling by my door
Sweet beverage shall be
And I will have a plenteous store
Of Honey from the tree.

"A little spot for herbs and roots
Will be my greatest care
And gathering these with fallen nuts
'Gainst winter's dearth prepare.

"Let winter come my Lute and I
When raves the snowy blast
Will weave a gentle lulaby
Until the storm is past.

"While on the hearth the branches blaze
And light my leaf-lined bower
I'll ne'er regret my world-past days
Nor envy wealth and power.

"I have a kingdom in my mind
My Fancy's wide domain
And gentle thoughts and visions kind
Shall be my serving train.

"There renounce all mortal love
Spirits O hear my vow!
No more shall tender passion move;
To be propitious now.

"And if this prayerful vow arise
All pleasing to your ears
And you accept my sacrifice;
Let some sure sign appear."

I scarce had ceased when rushed a blast
Through the black wood with rain;
My Lute afar from me was cast —
Its strings were snapt in twain.

I snatched it in my trembling fear
And fled the darksome dell.
No more I sought the forest drear:
Constrained 'mid men to dwell.

My gentle Lute I strung again:
It still had power to move. —
Again I struck the thrilling strain
Of tendernous and Love.

The maid I once believed so cold,
Listened and softly sighed,
And when I told her scorn of old
Two melting lips replied.

88.

The Man of Pride

He sat upon a rock that proudly rear'd
Upon the mountain's top; higher than aught around.
His brow bore lines, which were not those that years
Are wont to grave — but stronger deeper marks
Of thought, of suffering, and of passion's power —

His face was nobly formed; but pride sat stern
Upon its beauty, darkening it as though
A fiend there cast the shadow of his wing —

There he had come to die: scorning the world,
In which he long had toiled for preeminence
By trampling too, upon his fellow man
Whom he considered slave — and he had risen —
High, and had been cast down — but yet that spirit
    pride,
Could never be cut down — He left the world
He could not dominate — and fled to wilds
To be a monarch there; but pride is torture —
For in the wild the beasts would not obey,
The winds blew where they listed, and the storm
Beat fiercely e'en on him — He climbed the hill
It was a foolish thought — that he might stand
And look from high upon the world he hated,
He gazed upon it and he wished for power
To scatter lightenings into distant lands —

And in the fury of excited pride
Towards the clouds he raised an impious hand
To reach the thunderbolt and fell and died
By his own passion's lightening struck down.

89.

The Mountain Bird

Roused by the carol of the mountain bird
From dreams of earth and sorrow I awoke.
Uplifted by the blissful strains I heard
Bright Hope again upon my spirit broke:

"O bird!" I said "That warblest to the soul
And with wild musick through the summer long
Dost charm the orbèd days as on they roll
And makest the mountains listeners to thy song;

"Whence is the magic of thine artless strain?
Is it the effluence of a sinless breast: —
The gush of innocent joy untouched by pain, —
The beauteous language of a Spirit blessed?

"Sing on thou Heaven-taught Minstrel so thy song
May find the inmost chamber of my soul —
And echoing there its melody prolong
'Till death's dark billows o'er my bosom roll.

"If unto thee such melody is given,
Subject to Death and earth-born like to me,
The burthen of my song so full of Heaven,
What must the choral songs of Seraphs be — ?"

Catskill Mountain House

90.

The Mountain Bird

Roused by the matin of the mountain bird
From dreams of earth and sorrow I awoke.
Uplifted by the blissful strains I heard
Bright Hope again upon my spirit broke.

"O Bird!" I said, "that warblest to my soul
And with wild music through the summer long
Dost charm the orbèd days as on they roll
And makest the mountains listeners to thy song.

"Whence is the magic of thine artless strain?
Is it the effluence of a sinless breast —
The gush of innocent joy, untouched by pain
The mystic language of a spirit blest?

"Sing on thou Heaven-taught minstrel so thy song
May find the inmost chamber of my soul
And echoing there its melody prolong
'Till death's dark billows o'er my bosom roll.

"If unto thee such melody is givèn,
Subject to Death and earth-born like to me,
The burthen of thy song so full of Heaven,
What must the choral songs of Seraphs be?"

Catskill Mountain House

91.

To ——

When leaves seem trembling with delight
Upon the twilight sky
And eve-clouds in the purple light
Are wasting silently, —
When from the depth of some brown wood
The cataract's spray ascends,
Or in the clear and trembling flood
The moon its radiance blends,
That is the hour I think of thee —
For thou more beautiful than they
Canst gaze and feel like me,
But leaves, and clouds, and cataract's spray,
And water moon-lit tremblingly,
Feel not — nor lovible thoughts have they
To turn to one who wanders far **away.**

92.

To a Lock of Hair —

Best relic of the distant or the dead
Unchanged art thou by season, space or years;
O'er present thoughts thou hast the power to shed
The hues of by-gone days, and call our tears
From out their founts, in soft and soothing sorrow;
Revealing to our souls, those whom we love,
In a full keen remembrance — And we borrow
Through thee a light into the past, and move
Among friends dear to us, and learn to know
Our bosoms are not chilled by care and wrong
And *love* as they *have* loved — except the flow
Of their affection is *more* deep and strong —

Like to a lake whose icy bands are riven
By the soft breath of spring — it breaks away
And to the current power and strength are given
By that which bound it on the winter's day.

T. C.

93.

To CBT[1]

Hast thou forgotten me my friend
Me and the hours in social converse pass'd
When our glad spirits each supporting each
On the strong wings of sympathy upborne
Into the realms of extacy have soar'd —
Far, far, above the dense foul atmosphere
Of Worldly things — Hast thou forgotten me.
Me and our wanderings in the mountain's wilds
By those lone lakes that sleep so calm
Beneath the shadows of the piny hills —
Or that bleak cliff on which we stood amaz'd
And look'd upon the world beneath our feet,
And on the clouds huge rolling o'er our heads
And felt like spirits of the air sublime
Free and unfettered by our mortal bonds.
Hast thou forgotten too our deep commune
When night had hung o'er mountain top and vale
Her gloomy veil impervious, and had pour'd,
On every eye but ours, the balm of sleep.
Though darkness was around, our souls were light
Kindled by inspiration — and we had
Such views sublime of the great universe
And of its God as mortals seldom gain —
Hast thou forgotten me my friend
O no! it cannot cannot be; our souls
So many times have drunk from the same cup
Which nature held — that they are link'd
In hands which nought but death hath pow'r to break.

94.

To Spring

Not on dove-like pinions
    To thy wide dominions
        Spring thou doest come
But on the tempest's wing
Driving the Hoary Ring
An exile in Antartic wastes to roam.
Like Freedom when she shouteth
    "Tyrants shall fall"
And her banner flouteth
    O'er the crushed dungeon-wall,
And her foot trampleth on the Crowned wrong
    Fierce art thou Spring and wonderfully strong.
But the dreadful battle o'er
And winter struggleth no more,
And the Captive Lakes are free
And the flowerets on the lea;[1]
And the birds are praising thee
    Gentle as Freedom when
    Peace is restored to men,
    And Love with wide extended hands
Does sit the ruler of the lands.

95.

A reminiscence of my perish'd love
Shone softly o'er my mind
It came as moonlight on the grove
Or music on the wind —
It had a sweet regretful power
Like fragrance from a withered flower —

Ye visitations from the fading past,
  Spirits of departed joys,
When gloom and sadness overcast,
  Then to my soul arise
And be like sunshine on the grave
Of hopes I loved but could not save —
  Come as the twilight of the day
  Whose summer now is past away —

96.

A reminiscence of departed love
Shone softly o'er my mind
It came like moonlight on the grove;
Or music on the wind:
It had a sweet regretful power
Like fragrance from a withered flower.

Ye visitations from the fading past —
Spirits of departed joys!
When gloom and sadness overcast
Then to my soul arise,
And be like sunshine on the grave
Of hopes I reared but could not save —
Come as the twilight of the day
Whose splendor now is past away.

97.

A spell comes o'er th' excited soul whene'er
Soft music floats upon the breeze; all things
Do then inanimate or quick appear; to feel.

The insect on the winged sound seems borne
The bird is urged on its airy course; the bark
Is wafted on — mysteriously —

98.

How awful was the voice that came to Job
In the still night — that said "shall mortal man
Be more just than his God" — In robe mysterious
The spirit form was wrapp'd — Solemn, and slow
The words broke forth — and deep as is the roar
Of some vast, distant cataract, whose sound
Shakes the dark woods, the rocks, the hills around
And rises, sinks and thunders on the shore —

99.

How changeful is the cloud that flits along
From darkling crag to crag, to it belong
Nor fixedness nor rest, ever it moves
As vainly seeking some bright thing which loves —
Thus 'tis with one whose longing bosom beats
Lured on by beauty, but who never meets
The love-glance answering from a modest eye —
No murmuring assent and no responding sigh;
And finds with anguish none can love him well
Though in his bosom love would fainly dwell —

100.

O Nature my sole mistress unto thee
I turn again and wonder why my soul
Should ever seek for Beauty's smiles; to be
Deceived as they have aye[1] deceived — The bowl
Of love to me much bitterness doth hold —
Sweet smiles are oft but flowers gay
Hiding the rock forever hard and cold, —
But thy sweet smiles Nature ne'er betray.

101.

Take me Zephyr on thy wings
From the din of worldly things
Waft me to the mountains high
Take me Zephyr or I die —

Take me Zephyr to the roar
Of ocean dashing on its shore
Where no one hears its voice but I
Take me Zephyr or I die —

Take me Zephyr to some vale
Where solitude and peace prevail
Where mortal step is never nigh
Take me Zephyr or I die —

Take me Zephyr on thy wings
Where to th' Recluse nothing brings
A thought of man: there could I
Live in peace and peaceful die.

102.

Thy gloom O twilight suits my soul
For pensive sadness dwells with thee;
And deep thoughts rise by thy controul
Like swells upon a tranquil sea —

Yes! on the ocean of my mind
Which has been lash'd by the tempests rude
That are gone by; but leave behind
The silent heaving of the flood —

I wander slowly there to mark
The sunlit heavens fading fast
Like youth's own visions growing dark
Too lov'd, too beautiful to last —

There is a cloud upon the sky
And it hath ta'en the saddest hue
No kindred clouds are floating by
Sojourning in the trackless blue.

An emblem of my destiny,
In that low cloud perhaps I find
Companionless like it to be
When fortune's sun hath sad declin'd.

103.

'Tis all a dream: our joys, our fears
Our hopes a dream — The spirit hath existence
But now it sleeps, of its earthly sleep
These are the feverish visions — The waking time
Draws near, when all such ill-form'd phantasies
Shall flee away like night-clouds from the sun —
A morn shall dawn: a bright mid-day arrive
Then the reality of being shall be known
In the full glory of eternal life —

104.

Who breaks the silence of the night
With deep and desperate cry?
Who curses while the golden light
Is on the mountains high? —

    In a stone dungeon deep and dark
    A miserable wretch doth lie
    Who calls for vengeance, raves for love
    But praying cannot die —

    Three days within that rock bound cell
    Three summer days they short may seem
    To those who on the mountains dwell
    And watch the cloud's sunny beam —

But unto him whose fetters gall
Bound to the cold unpitying stone
Where light nor dew drop ever fall
Where earth's dank sweat at each loud groan
Is shaken from the shiney wall
Three days are centuries —

105.

Who that hath breathed on mountain top, where winds
Gush[1] **fresh from heaven — who that had proudly** stood
O'er the embattled cliff and watched the clouds;
Heave in extended tumult far below;
Or felt the torrent's spray dash on his cheek:
Can unregretful let his days consume
In tainted cities where the air is thick
And stagnant with impurity and hath
Been breathed and breathed again — amid the din
The daily darkness and the lasting strife —

REFERENCES

In his original manuscripts Cole wrote variant words and phrases in the following manner:

erring
"Told by my feeble tongue to mortal ears —"

All variants have been footnoted and are found in the reference material in this format:

1 feeble/erring.

1. THE TIMES, p. 31.
    1 beldame: old woman.
2. FANCY, p. 32.
    1 feeble/erring.
3. THE VISION OF LIFE, p. 34.
    1 ignus fatuus: a light seen at night moving over swamps or marshy places; popularly called "will-o-the-wisp," "jack-o-lantern."
    2 some evil power/as we approach.
    3 transformed/were changed.
5. TWILIGHT, p. 38.
    1 From a rough draft manuscript found in a verse notebook among poems dated 1825.
6. The night was calm. Clad in her mantle darkness . . . p. 39.
    1 Cerulean: sky-blue, azure.
    2 lay: a song or melody.
    3 refulgent: shining, glowing.
    4 recked: mattered.
7. FOR AN ALBUM, p. 44.
    1 Delia: In Greek mythology, Artemis, goddess of the moon, wild animals and hunting.
8. LINES ON LAKE GEORGE, p. 45.
    1 Lake George is located in the foothills of the Adirondack Mountains in eastern New York. This long, narrow lake was the scene of many bloody conflicts during the French and Indian Wars.

2 Horican: A fictitious name for Lake George used by James Fenimore Cooper in his Indian romances. In a footnote in THE LAST OF THE MOHICANS (1826) Cooper comments on the lake's attractive setting: "The beauties of Lake George are well known to every American tourist. In the height of the mountains which surround it, and in artificial accessories, it is inferior to the finest of the Swiss and Italian lakes, while in outline and purity of water it is fully their equal, and in the number and disposition of its isles and islets much superior to them altogether. There are said to be some hundreds of islands in a sheet of water less than thirty miles long. The narrows which connect what may be called, in truth, two lakes, are crowded with islands to such a degree as to leave passages between them frequently of only a few feet in width. The lake itself varies in breadth from one to three miles." (Riverside edition, note on p. 219.)

3 The Roman Catholic priests used the waters of Lake George for baptismal purposes. [T. C.]

4 The Massacre near Fort William Henry. [T. C.]

9. TO MOUNT WASHINGTON, p. 49.
   1 Highest peak of the White Mountains, New Hampshire.
   2 Cole spent several days sketching in the White Mountains in the fall of 1828. He took notes of the excursion on the blank leaves of his sketchbook.

10. NIAGARA, p. 50.
   1 iris: rainbow.
   2 Cole visited Niagara for the first time just before his departure for England in June, 1829.

11. Alas! he is a wretch who has no home . . . p. 52.
   1 On June 1, 1829, Cole sailed from New York for London, where he remained for nearly two years studying and practicing his art.
   2 will/can.

12. Let not the ostentatious gaud of art . . . p. 53.
   1 These lines were penned on the cover of a sketchbook (Noble, p. 75).

13. WRITTEN ON MY BIRTHDAY, FEB. 1, 1830, p. 54.
   1 Cole was residing in London at this time.

2 See John Milton's 1637 pastoral elegy "Lycidas," in which the poet expresses his thoughts on the nature of true fame.

3 The pictures of the Falls of Niagara and Elijah were the first I ever sent to Exhibition in England, are in the gallery of the British Institution; but hung so that they cannot be seen. [T. C.]

4 Subsequent to his return from Europe, Cole wrote in a letter to William Dunlap that he was disappointed with England: "I found myself a nameless, noteless individual, in the midst of an immense, selfish multitude. I did not expect much, scarcely anything more than to have an opportunity of studying, and showing some of my pictures in the public exhibitions. . . ; but the pictures I sent . . . were, without exception, hung in the worst places so that my acquaintances had a difficulty in knowing them." (Noble, p. 79.) Noble does not cite the date of this letter, nor is the manuscript to be found among the New York State Library Papers.

15. I see the green Fiesole arise . . . p. 58.
    1 An ancient town in Italy, now a suburb of Florence, set on top of a large hill.
    2 One of the longest rivers in Italy.
    3 Fiesole and Arno both are fam'd in song/Arno, Fiesole — both famed in song.

16. A lonely cloud is flitting round the brow . . . p. 59.
    1 When earthly sorrow cannot follow me./When sorrow's shadowy clouds can never be.

17. The eager vessel flies the broken surge . . . p. 60.
    1 This poem anticipates Cole's 1840 series of paintings, *The Voyage of Life,* which deals with the same theme. An alternate version, dated 1834, appears on the facing page. See also "Life's Pilgrimage," p. 37, and "The Voyage of Life," p. 145.

18. The eager vessel flies the broken surge . . . p. 61.
    1 storms/waves.

19. LINES WRITTEN AFTER A WALK ON [A] BEAUTIFUL MORNING IN NOVEMBER, p. 62.
    1 Like William Wordsworth in his 1798 poem "Lines Composed a Few Miles above Tintern Abbey," Cole is here concerned with the absorptions and worship of the true romantic.

23. THE PAINTER'S LAMENTATION, p. 69.
> 1 Originally, "The Painter's Lamentation of Love," but Cole deleted the last two words in his final version.
> 2 Alban Hills: remains of an extinct volcano, Laziale, near Rome.
> 3 There was a temple formerly on the summit of Mont Albana — [T. C.]
> 4 Hannibal it is said encamped with his army on a plain a little below the summit of M Albana, near a village now called Rocca de papa — [T. C.]
> 5 Campagna: the plain around Rome.
> 6 Sracte: i.e., Soracte, a mountain conspicuous enough to be seen from Rome.
> 7 sabine: outside Rome.
> 8 Dated from a rough draft manuscript.

26. I sigh not for a stormless clime . . . p. 74.
> 1 Cole's Journal, Jan. 25, 1835: "My soul dwells in a mortal tenement and feels the influence of the elements—I would not dwell where tempests never come for they bring beauty in their train."
> 2 Hath made/Doth make.

31. Though time has sadden'd every thought . . . p. 80.
> 1 Cole's Journal, Aug. 25, 1835: "I am most happy when I can escape most from the world. The longer I live in it, the more its common cares and troubles seem to claim me. Nothing makes me so melancholy as that which prevents me from the pursuit of my art."

32. Winter had fled into his northern home . . . p. 81.
> 1 wonted: accustomed.
> 2 Luman Reed (1787-1836), the foremost art patron of his generation and Cole's most generous sponsor.

34. LINES OCCASIONED BY THE DEATH OF MR. LUMAN REED, p. 83.
> 1 During his friendship with Cole, Reed commissioned many of the artist's works, among them *The Course of Empire*. Elliot S. Vesell has summarized Reed's role as a benefactor to American artists: "He was a prototype of the merchant patron who felt it a pleasure both to offer 'encouragement and support to better men than myself' and to share in the patriotic enterprise of delineating the characteristics of American nature.

Instead of attempting to influence the artists by telling them what to paint, as Gilmor did, Reed bought what they produced and encouraged them by loans, financing European tours, employing members of their families, and reassuring them when their spirits sank" (Noble, p. 319).

2 Cosimo de' Medici (1389-1464), banker, statesman and patron of art and literature; head of the Florentine Republic.

3 Lorenzo de' Medici (1449-1492), Prince of Florence, statesman, poet, scholar and patron of art and literature.

4 Florence, Italy: the Italian name.

35. SONG OF THE SPIRIT OF THE MOUNTAIN, p. 87.

1 aye: always.

2 Schroon Mountain, N. Y.

3 Dated from rough draft.

36. The wight who climbs the mountain's gleaming side . . . p. 89.

1 wight: person.

37. WRITTEN IN AUTUMN, p. 90.

1 sere: withered.

2 aye: always

3 rills: little brooks, rivulets.

39. On the frore shadow of yon mountain-steep . . . p. 93.

1 frore: frosty, frozen.

40. Thine early hopes are fading one by one . . . p. 94.

1 chaunt: chant.

2 A lasting Day shall dawn in the resplendent East/A brighter day shall dawn in the Eternal East.

41. Thine early Hopes are fading one by one . . . p. 95.

1 murmuring/struggling.

2 Undated manuscript.

42. And shall I halt midway in my career . . . p. 96.

1 Cole's Journal, July 1, 1838: "The longer I pursue my art, the more my experience, and the more cultivated my eye becomes, the more impotent is my skill to represent on canvass the ever-varying features of nature. And instead of appearing to approach nearer to perfection in imitation, I feel to be removed farther and farther away until at times I am overwhelmed by a melancholy fear that I am retrograding—that my season of improvement is past."

2 Fane: temple, church.

43. Thou frail and feeble vine . . . p. 97.

    1 Cole's Journal, July 22, 1838: "There is a climbing plant attached to a large oak in our Grove, which I have watched from year to year. In spring it puts forth a few leaves and spreads a few green tendrils; but winter entirely blasts them and the slender woody stem, to all appearances, remains without any increase of size."

44. I saw a cave of sable depth profound . . . p. 98.

    1 sable/gulphy.

    2 Probably Schoharie Cave, near Albany, which Cole visited on Oct. 9, 1838. He describes the trip in his journal on this date.

    3 Cole finished the poem before the end of the month and sent a copy to Dr. George Ackerly, his brother-in-law, for his comments.

45. SONNET, p. 99.

    1 adamant: A very hard stone or substance.

    2 Cole may have been referring to the events which followed the revolt of William Lyon MacKenzie, the Canadian insurgent leader, who in the fall of 1837 sought to lead an insurrection against the Crown. Loyalist Canadians easily defeated the rebellion, but a United States vessel, the *Caroline,* which had carried supplies to the rebels, was subsequently attacked while at anchor in New York by a group of British who were angered at this breach of neutrality. The destruction of an American ship in its own waters was interpreted as an act of war and inflamed the passion of Americans in general and New Yorkers in particular. President Van Buren and Governor Marcy kept the peace, but the effort cost them and their party much popular support. Throughout most of 1838, outraged American patriots attempted to organize for an attack on Canada. Although several minor skirmishes resulted, no invasion was carried out.

    The conduct of the United States government in the whole matter was sharply criticized and New York voters expressed their condemnation of the administration and its party by electing, in 1838, William H. Seward governor over William L. Marcy.

46. THE COMPLAINT OF THE FOREST, p. 100.

    1 Cole was disturbed that the forests were disappearing. In a letter to Luman Reed (Mar. 26, 1836, Catskill) Cole complains that trees were being destroyed to make way for a railroad. See also Cole's 1834 poem, "On seeing that a favorite tree of the Author's had been cut down —" which deals with this subject on a smaller scale.

    2 Empyrean: the highest heaven; among Christian poets, the abode of God.

    3 On the shores of the small lake near the Catskill M House in early June are found white violets of exquisite perfume. [T. C.]

    4 bourne: domain.

    5 Thebes: an ancient city in Egypt on the Nile.

    6 Persepolis: a ruined city in southern Iran; ancient capital of Persia.

    7 Echoes: i.e., Echo

    8 Hyrcania: a province in the ancient Persian empire.

    9 The cedar of Lebanon is the best known of the cedars because of its frequent appearance in art and literature as a symbol of power and longevity.

    10 Uranus: in Greek mythology, a god who was the personification and original ruler of the universe; name of the seventh planet of the sun.

    11 Lazuli: an azure-blue, opaque, semi-precious stone.

    12 King Ferdinand IV of Spain united Aragon and Castile by marriage and absorbed Granada into the Spanish empire.

    13 Xerxes: king of Persia whose invasion of Greece in 483 B. C. ended in defeat at Salamis in 480.

    14 Mammon: the false god of riches and avarice.

    15 Volga: a river in the European U. S. S. R.

    16 wimpling: rippling.

    17 bosky: woody.

47. THE LAMENT OF THE FOREST, p. 107.

    1 Published in THE KNICKERBOCKER, XVII (May, 1841), 516-519. No complete manuscript exists. James T. Callow notes that Bryant was asked to revise the poem before publication by editor Lewis G. Clark. Cole agreed to this, and "Lament" was subsequently published. (KINDRED SPIRITS:

48. Oft when o'er Earth is spread the gloomy shade . . . p. 113.

    1 An undated poem found in Cole's Journal among the January-May, 1838, entries.

49. Why do ye count your little months, your years . . . p. 114.

    1 Cole's Journal, Dec. 26, 1839: "The latest footsteps of the year are now being impressed on the unstable, sandy beach of time—that shore which skirts the ocean of eternity. It is a narrow shore that man treads. Before him spread thick mists and darkness: and ever and anon, we hear the plunge of some one who has fallen into the deep. But let us not fear. It is the corporeal part of man that sinks. The soul soars over that vast sea, and finds a fitter dwelling place."

50. Upon the bosom of the infant year . . . p. 115.

    1 Cole's son, Theodore, was born Jan. 1, 1838.

    2 coeval: contemporary.

51. THE DIAL, p. 116.

    1 gnomon: a column on a sundial that casts a shadow indicating the time of day.

52. BIRDSNEST, p. 117.

    1 th' unfading/Hope's holy.

54. BIRTHDAY, p. 119.

    1 Written to Maria, Cole's wife.

55. THE SUMMER DAYS ARE ENDED, p. 120.

    1 Entitled "Autumn" on the rough draft manuscript.

    2 harshly/loudly.

    3 barren/frozen.

56. THE SUMMER DAYS ARE ENDED, p. 123.

    1 Published under the name "Pictor" in THE KNICKERBOCKER, XVI (Dec., 1840), pp. 504-505.

57. WRITTEN UPON AN AUTUMNAL LEAF, p. 126.

    1 sybil or sibyl: any of certain women consulted as prophetesses or oracles by the ancient Greeks or Romans.

    2 The 1840 date I have assigned is an approximate one. The poem could have been written as early as November, 1836, when Cole married Maria Bartow. The source for the date is

poem 53 (Though snows enwrap the mountain's head . . .),
line 5, "Maria this fond wish of mine," which is nearly
identical with line 7, "Maria, no fond wish of thine."

58. ON ANOTHER, p. 127.

    1 Found on the same manuscript page as "Written on an
Autumnal Leaf" which I have dated 1840.

59. Like a cloud on the brow of a mountain . . . p. 128.

    1 Cole's Journal, Jan. 1, 1841: "The last day of each year comes
on us, as it were, by surprise; we look back astonished that
another year is gone—In what a small compass seems the year
to be comprissed; for memory in a few minutes may review the
avocations—scenes—incidents and occurances that occupied
us through 365 days."

60. This day hath closed another of my years . . . p. 130.

    1 ken: range of vision.

61. WINDS, p. 131.

    1 Published under the name "Pictor" in THE KNICKERBOCKER,
XVII (May, 1841), p. 339.

    2 Himmalah: Himalaya.

    3 erst: long ago.

62. AUTUMN, p. 132.

    1 Untitled manuscript.

    2 silent/softly.

63. AUTUMN, p. 133.

    1 This poem was found on the same manuscript page as "Lago
Maggiore," which is dated 1842.

64. MT. ETNA, p. 134.

    1 Cole describes his ascent of Mt. Etna, the volcanic mountain in
eastern Sicily, in his journal of May 9, 1842.

    2 Proserpina: in Roman mythology, the daughter of Ceres and
wife of Pluto, god of the underworld.

    3 Charybdis: a whirlpool off the coast of Sicily, opposite the
rock Scylla.

65. LAGO MAGGIORE, p. 136.

    1 A lake in Switzerland and northwestern Italy which Cole passed
on his way from Italy to England.

66. LIFE'S PILGRIMAGE, p. 137.

1 Compare this allegorical treatment of the theme of life's perilous journey with John Bunyan's THE PILGRIM'S PROGRESS (1678) and with William Cullen Bryant's "The Passage of Time." See also Cole's 1844 poem, "The Voyage of Life" (p. 145), and his 1840 allegorical painting series of the same title.

67. A SUNSET, p. 140.

1 Written in memory of Washington Allston (1779-1843), the outstanding landscape painter in America during the first two decades of the 19th century.

68. ON A SUNSET SKY, p. 141.

1 Entitled "A Sunset" on the rough draft manuscript.

69. WINTER, p. 142.

1 And 'neath the ice-heaps seeks its dismal way./And seeks 'neath heaped ice its dismal way.

2 steadfast/firm.

3 A fragment of this poem was found in Cole's journal for March, 1843, in which he describes a trip to the Falls of Caterskill taken the month before.

70. WINTER, p. 143.

1 darksome/dismal.

2 See note 3, poem 69.

71. THE VOYAGE OF LIFE, p. 145.

1 According to Louis L. Noble, Cole biographer, these lines were written as a solace for Cole's grief upon the death of his friend and colleague, Cornelius Ver Bryck (1813-1844). The poem is a translation, in heroic verse, of Cole's allegorical series, *The Voyage of Life*, which was completed in the fall of 1840.

2 antre: cave, cavern.

3 verge/brow.

4 Hours: in Greek mythology, the goddesses of the seasons, justice, order and peace.

5 like/as.

6 Zephyr: soft, gentle breeze.

7 cerulean: sky-blue azure.

8 Taormina: a town on the east coast of Sicily (ancient Tauromenium).

9 Etna [T. C.]

10 Torre del Filosofo, a Roman ruin believed to commemorate the ascent of Etna by the Emperor Hadrian.

11 (A)eolian: carried or produced by the wind.

12 fane: temple, church.

13 wondering/lost enraptured.

14 wrack: a broken mass of clouds or vapor.

15 sky/air.

16 tyrannic/tyrannous

17 Lethe: in Greek and Roman mythology, the river of forgetfulness, flowing through Hades, whose waters produced a loss of memory in those who drank of it; hence oblivion, forgetfulness.

18 Siloam: in the Bible, a spring and pool outside Jerusalem (John 9:7).

19 dun: a dull, grayish brown.

20 fulgent: bright, radiant.

21 seraphic: angelic.

22 reft: seized.

23 reach/gain.

24 hies: speeds, hastens.

73. THE MARCH OF TIME, p. 162.
   1 frore: frosty, frozen.

74. THE MARCH OF TIME, p. 164.
   1 sound/speak.

77. ALONE YET NOT ALONE, p. 168.
   1 John 15:1-32. [T. C.]

78. A PAINTER, p. 169.
   1 chamber/study.
   2 match/grasp.

80. LIFE, p. 171.
   1 span of years/vale of tears.

82. LINES SUGGESTED BY A PICTURE PAINTED BY WEIR, IN WHICH A LADY IS SEEN SITTING AT A WINDOW GAZING ON THE SEA, WHILST A YOUTH AT HER SIDE IS PLAYING THE GUITAR, p. 173.
   1 Robert Walter Weir (1803-1889), American painter of historical subjects and landscapes.

83. LINES SUGGESTED BY A VOYAGE UP THE HUDSON ON A MOONLIGHT NIGHT, p. 174.

    1 fay: fairy.

93. TO CBT, p. 190.

    1 Charles B. Trego (1794-1874), a Pennsylvania geographer and once treasurer of the American Philosophical Association. No reference to Trego is made by Cole's biographer, Louis L. Noble. Most likely, Trego met Cole during the artist's residence in Philadelphia (1823-25).

    There exist four letters which Trego wrote to Cole from Philadelphia during 1826-28. In his letter of July 18, 1828, Trego refers to their recent sojourn in the Catskill Mountains, where Cole taught him to "muse on Nature with a poet's eye."

94. TO SPRING, p. 191.

    1 lea: meadow, grassy field.

100. O Nature my sole mistress unto thee . . . p. 197.

    1 aye: always.

105. Who that hath breathed on mountain top, where winds . . . p. 202.

    1 gush/are.

BIBLIOGRAPHY

Alison, Archibald (1830) ESSAYS ON THE NATURE AND PRINCIPLES OF TASTE: New York.

Andrews, Wayne, and McCoy, Garnett (1965) *Romantic America and the Discovery of Nature, 1825-1860,* ART IN AMERICA, LIII, 38-53.

Barker, Virgil (1950) AMERICAN PAINTING: HISTORY AND INTERPRETATION: New York.

Baur, John I. H. (1953) AMERICAN PAINTING IN THE NINETEENTH CENTURY: New York.

Beach, Joseph Warren (1956) THE CONCEPT OF NATURE IN NINETEENTH-CENTURY ENGLISH POETRY: New York.

Beard, James F., Jr. (1954) *Cooper and his Artistic Contemporaries,* in JAMES FENIMORE COOPER: A RE-APPRAISAL: Papers of the New York State Historical Association Annual Meeting, 1951: Cooperstown.

Benjamin, S. G. W. (1880) ART IN AMERICA: New York.

Born, Wolfgang (1948) AMERICAN LANDSCAPE PAINTING: New Haven.

Bryant, William Cullen (1848) A FUNERAL ORATION, OCCASIONED BY THE DEATH OF THOMAS COLE, DELIVERED BEFORE THE NATIONAL ACADEMY OF DESIGN, NEW YORK, MAY, 4, 1848: New York.

Burke, Edmund (1844) A PHILOSOPHICAL INQUIRY INTO THE ORIGIN OF OUR IDEAS OF THE SUBLIME AND BEAUTIFUL: New York.

Callow, James T. (1967) KINDRED SPIRITS: KNICKERBOCKER WRITERS AND AMERICAN ARTISTS, 1807-1855: Chapel Hill.

Charvat, William (1936) THE ORIGINS OF AMERICAN CRITICAL THOUGHT, 1810-1835: Philadelphia.

Cole, Thomas (September, 1840) *A Letter to Critics on the Art of Painting,* THE KNICKERBOCKER MAGAZINE, XVI, 230-233.

Cole, Thomas (May 14, 1825) *Emma Moreton, A West Indian Tale,* SATURDAY EVENING POST, IV, 1-2.

Cole, Thomas (January, 1836) *Essay on American Scenery,* THE AMERICAN MONTHLY MAGAZINE, I, 1-12.

Cole, Thomas (May, 1841) *Lecture Delivered before the Catskill Lyceum on April 1, 1841,* THE NORTHERN LIGHT, I, 25-26.

Cole, Thomas (October 31, 1846) *Letter about Frescoes,* THE CHURCHMAN, XVI, 138.

Cole, Thomas (December 5, 1846) *Letter about Frescoes,* THE CHURCHMAN, XVI, 158.

Cole, Thomas (June, 1841) *The Lament of the Forest,* THE KNICKERBOCKER MAGAZINE, XVII, 516-519.

Cole, Thomas (December, 1840) *The Summer Days are Ended,* THE KNICKERBOCKER MAGAZINE, XVI, 504-505.

Cole, Thomas (February, 1844; March, 1844) *Sicilian Scenery and Antiquities,* THE KNICKERBOCKER MAGAZINE, XXIII, 103-113; 236-244.

Cole, Thomas (May, 1841) *Winds,* THE KNICKERBOCKER MAGAZINE, XVII, 399.

Cummings, Thomas S. (1865) HISTORIC ANNUALS OF THE NATIONAL ACADEMY OF DESIGN: Philadelphia.

Denny, Margaret, and Gilman, William H., eds. (1950) THE AMERICAN WRITER AND THE EUROPEAN TRADITION: Minneapolis.

Dunlap, William (1918) A HISTORY OF THE RISE AND PROGRESS OF THE ARTS OF DESIGN IN THE UNITED STATES, ed. Frank W. Bayley and Charles E. Goodspeed. 3 vols.: Boston.

Fairchild, Hoxie N. (1931) THE ROMANTIC QUEST: New York.

Flexner, James T. (1962) THAT WILDER IMAGE: THE PAINTING OF AMERICA'S NATIVE SCHOOL FROM THOMAS COLE TO WINSLOW HOMER: Boston.

Forester, Norman (1950) NATURE IN AMERICAN LITERATURE: New York.

Forester, Norman, ed. (1928) THE REINTERPRETATION OF AMERICAN LITERATURE: New York.

Francis, Henry S. (1937) *Thomas Cole: Painter of the Catskill Mountains,* THE BULLETIN OF THE CLEVELAND MUSEUM OF ART, XXIV, 113-116.

Gerdts, William H., Jr. (1967) *Cole's Painting: "After the Temptation,"* in STUDIES ON THOMAS COLE, AN

AMERICAN ROMANTICIST, 103-111. Baltimore Museum of Art ANNUAL II, 103-111: Baltimore.

Goodrich, Lloyd (1938) A CENTURY OF AMERICAN LANDSCAPE PAINTING, 1800-1900 (exhibition catalog, Whitney Museum of American Art): New York.

Goodrich, Lloyd (1966) THREE CENTURIES OF AMERICAN ART: New York.

Green, Samuel M. (1966) AMERICAN ART: A HISTORICAL SURVEY: New York.

Hale, Edward E., Jr. (1910) *American Scenery in Cooper's Novels,* SEWANEE REVIEW, XVIII, 317-322.

Hale, Edward E., Jr. (1916) *The Early Art of Thomas Cole,* ART IN AMERICA, IV, 22-40.

Harris, Neil (1966) THE ARTIST IN AMERICAN SOCIETY: THE FORMATIVE YEARS, 1790-1860: New York.

Huntington, Daniel (1850) *Character of Thomas Cole,* THE LITERARY WORLD, VI, 377-378.

Huth, Hans (1957) NATURE AND THE AMERICAN: THREE CENTURIES OF CHANGING ATTITUDES: Berkeley.

Isham, Samuel (1944) THE HISTORY OF AMERICAN PAINTING: New York.

Jones, Howard M. (1944) IDEAS IN AMERICA: Cambridge, Mass.

Jones, Howard M. (1952) *James Fenimore Cooper and the Hudson River School,* MAGAZINE OF ART, XLV, 243-251.

Jones, Howard M. (1952) *Prose and Pictures: James Fenimore Cooper,* TULANE STUDIES IN ENGLISH, III, 133-154.

LaBudde, Kenneth J. (1954) *The Mind of Thomas Cole,* Unpublished Ph.D. dissertation: University of Minnesota.

LaBudde, Kenneth J. (1958) *The Rural Earth: Sylvan Bliss,* AMERICAN QUARTERLY, X, 142-153.

Larkin, Oliver W. (1960) ART AND LIFE IN AMERICA rev. ed.: New York.

Lesley, Everett P., Jr. (1949) *Some Clues to Thomas Cole,* MAGAZINE OF ART, XLII, 42-48.

Lesley, Parker (1942) *Thomas Cole and the Romantic Sensibility,* THE ART QUARTERLY, V, 199-221.

Lewis, E. Anna (1855) *Art and Artists of America: Thomas Cole, N. A.,* GRAHAM'S MAGAZINE, XLVI, 330-341.

Lillie, Mrs. L. C. (1890) *Two Phases of American Art,* HARPER'S NEW MONTHLY MAGAZINE, LXXX, 206-216.

McCoubrey, John W. (1965) AMERICAN ART 1700-1960: SOURCES AND DOCUMENTS: Englewood Cliffs.

Mendelowitz, Daniel M. (1960) A HISTORY OF AMERICAN ART: New York.

Merritt, Howard S. (1969) THOMAS COLE (exhibition catalog, Memorial Art Gallery of the University of Rochester, Munson-Williams-Proctor Institute, Albany Institute of History and Art, and the Whitney Museum of American Art): Rochester.

Miller, Lillian B. (1967) *Painting, Sculpture, and the National Character, 1815-1860,* THE JOURNAL OF AMERICAN HISTORY, LIII, 696-707.

Miller, Perry (1955) *The Romantic Dilemma in American Nationalism and the Concept of Nature,* THE HARVARD THEOLOGICAL REVIEW, XLVIII, 239-253.

Miller, Ralph N. (1956) *Thomas Cole and Alison's Essays on Taste,* NEW YORK HISTORY, XXXVII, 281-299.

Morgan, Charles H., and Toole, Margaret C. (1951) *Notes on the Early Hudson River School,* ART IN AMERICA, XXXIX, 161-185.

Nash, Roderick (1967) WILDERNESS AND THE AMERICAN MIND: New Haven.

Nathan, Walter L. (1940) *Thomas Cole and the Romantic Landscape,* in ROMANTICISM IN AMERICA, ed. George Boas: Baltimore.

Noble, Louis L. (1964) THE LIFE AND WORKS OF THOMAS COLE, ed. Elliot S. Vesell: Cambridge, Mass.

Orians, G. Harrison (1953) *The Rise of Romanticism,* in TRANSITIONS IN AMERICAN LITERARY HISTORY, ed. Harry H. Clark: Durham.

Richardson, Edgar P. AMERICAN ROMANTIC PAINTING, ed. Robert Freund.

Richardson, Edgar P. (1956) PAINTING IN AMERICA: THE STORY OF 450 YEARS: New York.

Richardson, Edgar P. (1956) *The Romantic Genius of Thomas Cole,* ART NEWS, LV, 43, 52.

Ringe, Donald A. (1958) *James Fenimore Cooper and Thomas Cole: An Analogous Technique,* AMERICAN LITERATURE, XXX, 26-36.

Ringe, Donald A. (1954) *Kindred Spirits: Bryant and Cole,* AMERICAN QUARTERLY, VI, 233-244.

Ringe, Donald A. (1960) *Painting as Poem in the Hudson River Aesthetic,* AMERICAN QUARTERLY, XII, 71-83.

Sanford, Charles L. (1967) *The Concept of the Sublime in the Works of Thomas Cole and William Cullen Bryant,* AMERICAN LITERATURE, XXVIII, 434-448.

Schmitt, Evelyn L. (1953) *Two American Romantics— Thomas Cole and William Cullen Bryant,* ART IN AMERICA, XLI, 61-68.

Sears, Clara E. (1947) HIGHLIGHTS AMONG THE HUDSON RIVER ARTISTS: Cambridge, Mass.

Seaver, Esther I. (1948) THOMAS COLE, 1801-1848, ONE HUNDRED YEARS LATER (exhibition catalog, Wadsworth Atheneum and the Whitney Museum of American Art): Hartford.

Sedgwick, William E. (1953) *The Materials for an American Literature: A Critical Problem of the Early Nineteenth Century,* HARVARD STUDIES AND NOTES IN PHILOSOPHY AND LITERATURE, XVII, 141-162.

Soby, James T., and Miller, Dorothy C. (1943) ROMANTIC PAINTING IN AMERICA: New York.

Spencer, Benjamin T. (1967) THE QUEST FOR NATIONALITY: AN AMERICAN LITERARY CAMPAIGN: Syracuse.

Spiller, Robert E. (1947) *Critical Standards in the American Romantic Movement,* COLLEGE ENGLISH, VIII, 344-352.

Spiller, Robert E. (1967) THE AMERICAN LITERARY REVOLUTION, 1783-1837: New York.

Sweet, Frederick A. (1945) THE HUDSON RIVER SCHOOL AND THE EARLY AMERICAN LANDSCAPE TRADITION (exhibition catalog, Art Institute of Chicago and the Whitney Museum of American Art): Chicago.

Taylor, Walter F. (1936) A HISTORY OF AMERICAN LETTERS: New York.

Tuckerman, Henry T. (1882) AMERICAN ARTIST LIFE: New York.

Van Zandt, Roland (1966) THE CATSKILL MOUNTAIN HOUSE: New Brunswick.

Wallach, Alan P. (1968) *Cole, Byron, and the Course of Empire,* THE ART BULLETIN, L, 375-379.

Whitcomb, Selden L. (1893-94) *Nature in Early American Literature,* SEWANEE REVIEW, II, 159-179.

Woolley, Mary E. (1898) *The Development of the Love of Romantic Scenery in America,* AMERICAN HISTORICAL REVIEW, III, 56-66.

ABOUT THE EDITOR

THOMAS COLE'S POETRY is an outgrowth of Marshall B. Tymn's dissertation on "The Nature Poetry of Thomas Cole" for the Doctor of Philosophy degree in American culture which he was awarded by the University of Michigan in 1970.

Born December 11, 1937, he was an Eagle Scout and served as a medical corpsman in the U. S. Navy 1957-59. He was graduated from Wayne State University, Detroit, in 1962, and received the Master's degree in English from the same institution in 1964.

Tymn's fields of special study have been linguistics and American literature. He has taught at Wisconsin State University at Stevens Point, at Eastern Michigan University, Ypsilanti, where he holds an assistant Professorship, and at an English Language Institute of the University of Michigan. Now on leave from Eastern Michigan, he is serving as an associate professor at the University of the Americas, Puebla, Mexico.

He also has done research in the application of transformational theory to the teaching of eighth grade grammar on a grant from Wisconsin State University, and has served as a consultant to the Metropolitan Linguistics Society, a group of Detroit area secondary and college teachers.

A man of varied interests, Dr. Tymn is a jazz buff and trumpet player, and published "A Selected Bibliography of the Boston Classicists" in the *Music Journal* in 1970. He is also an amateur astronomer and an avid science fiction fan, as well as a scuba diver.

His wife, Darlene, who assisted in transcribing the Cole manuscripts, holds a Bachelor's degree in English from the University of Michigan.